QuickCook

QuickCook
Student

Recipes by Jo McAuley

Every dish, three ways—you choose!
30 minutes | 20 minutes | 10 minutes

An Hachette UK Company
www.hachette.co.uk

First published in Great Britain in 2013 by Hamlyn,
a division of Octopus Publishing Group Ltd.
Endeavour House, 189 Shaftesbury Avenue
London WC2H 8JY
www.octopusbooks.co.uk
www.octopusbooksusa.com

Distributed in the US by Hachette Book Group USA
237 Park Avenue, New York NY 10017 USA

Distributed in Canada by Canadian Manda Group
165 Dufferin Street, Toronto, Ontario, Canada M6K 3H6

ISBN 978-0-600-62701-2

Printed and bound in China.

10 9 8 7 6 5 4 3 2 1

Standard level spoon and cup measurements are used in all recipes.

Ovens should be preheated to the specified temperature. If using a convection oven,
follow the manufacturer's instructions for adjusting the time and temperature. Broilers
should also be preheated.

This book includes dishes made with nuts and nut derivatives. It is advisable for those
with known allergic reactions to nuts and nut derivatives and those who may be
potentially vulnerable to these allergies, such as pregnant and nursing mothers, people
with weakened immune systems, the elderly, babies, and children, to avoid dishes made
with nuts and nut oils.

It is also prudent to check the labels of prepared ingredients for the possible inclusion
of nut derivatives.

The United States Department of Agriculture (USDA) advises that eggs should not be
consumed raw. This book contains some dishes made with raw or lightly cooked eggs. It
is prudent for more vulnerable people, such as pregnant and nursing mothers, people with
weakened immune systems, the elderly, babies, and young children, to avoid uncooked or
lightly cooked dishes made with eggs.

Contents

Introduction

30 20 10—Quick, Quicker, Quickest

This book offers a new and flexible approach to planning for busy cooks, letting you choose the recipe option that best fits the time you have available. Inside, you will find 360 dishes that will inspire and motivate you to get cooking every day of the year. All the recipes take a maximum of 30 minutes to cook. Some take as little as 20 minutes, and, amazingly, many take only 10 minutes. With a little preparation, you can easily try out one new recipe from this book each night and slowly you will be able to build a wide and exciting portfolio of recipes to suit your needs.

How Does it Work?

Every recipe in the QuickCook series can be cooked one of three ways—a 30-minute version, a 20-minute version, or a superquick-and-easy 10-minute version. At the beginning of each chapter, you'll find recipes listed by time. Choose a dish based on how much time you have and turn to that page.

You'll find the main recipe in the middle of the page accompanied by a beautiful photograph, as well as two time-variation recipes below.

If you enjoy your chosen dish, why not go back and cook the other time-variation options at a later date? So if you liked the 30-minute Margherita Tart, but only have 10 minutes this time around, you'll find a way to cook it using quick ingredients or clever shortcuts.

If you love the ingredients and flavors of the 10-minute Citrus Chicken Salad, why not try something more substantial, such as the 20-minute Citrus Chicken Couscous, or be inspired to make a more elaborate version, such as the Citrus Baked Chicken? Alternatively, browse through all 360 delicious recipes, find something that catches your eye—then cook the version that fits your time frame.

Or, for easy inspiration, turn to the gallery on pages 12–19 to get an instant overview by themes, such as Twelve Ways with Poultry or Twelve Ways with Bacon and Sausage.

QuickCook Online

To make life even easier, you can use the special code on each recipe page to e-mail yourself a recipe card for printing, or e-mail a text-only shopping list to your phone. Go to www.hamlynquickcook.com and enter the recipe code at the bottom of each page.

STU-BRAI-REP

Student Meals

Becoming a student is not just about academic qualifications. It's also about learning how to survive on your own, which involves learning to cook and manage a tight grocery budget. And while a diet of fast food may seem like the quickest, cheapest, and easiest option, it is actually a false economy— it will not satisfy your hunger for as long as a home-cooked meal and can leave you feeling sluggish at best, unwell at worst. Instead, fuel your body for longer with healthy, inexpensive meals. Search through the delicious recipes in this book to find those that tempt you. There are dishes suitable for any occasion, be it a filling meal after sports training or a fun, home-cooked dinner with friends, and there's an entire chapter dedicated to feeding your brain as well as your stomach, using ingredients that are known to aid concentration.

There is no reason why cooking should feel like a chore. The following tips will help you make it more of a pleasure and stretch your budget to provide you with delicious and healthy meals.

Shopping Tips

Skillful shopping will make your pennies go further and keep your belly filled for longer. Plan your week's meals ahead, then write a list of the ingredients you'll need—and stick to it. It's easy to blow your budget on tempting treats and lavish ingredients without having bought the staples. And avoid walking around a supermarket when you are feeling hungry, which is a recipe for disaster!

Buy dried and canned goods in bulk when you can because it works out cheaper in the long run. Ethnic stores often sell economy size bags of dry produce, such as rice and couscous, and may also sell fresh produce more cheaply than supermarkets. Take advantage of supermarket promotions (such as buy-one-get-one-free offers), but only if the produce can be stored for a long time and if you will actually use it (instead of letting it rot in the cupboard). Check out local farmers' markets toward the end of trading to pick up great bargains. You may need to do some adventurous cooking with whatever ingredients you end with, which is a great opportunity for some kitchen adventures!

The Staples

If you always have a supply of useful ingredients on hand, you'll save time on your shopping trips and will always have the ingredients to whip up at least a few meals. Refer to the list here and stock up on these useful items.

When the funds are running especially low, a few pantry essentials can provide you with a supercheap meal. Although a bowl of pasta with a pat of butter and seasoning is unimaginative, it is a filling emergency standby meal. You'll be surprised how even the cheapest of ingredients can be used to make a fantastic feast when you are hungry and broke.

In the cupboard

- cooking oil (olive, vegetable, sesame)
- canned tomatoes
- canned beans (cannellini beans, baked beans, kidney beans, chickpeas, green lentils)
- canned fish (tuna, mackerel, salmon, sardines, anchovies)
- canned vegetables (peas, corn kernels)
- rice (long-grain, risotto)
- couscous
- pasta (a selection of shapes)
- noodles (rice, egg)
- bulgur wheat
- rolled oats
- dried fruits (apricots, raisins)
- nuts (walnuts, almonds, hazelnuts)
- sunflower seeds
- flour (all-purpose)
- cornstarch
- baking powder
- vanilla extract
- sugar (granulated, brown)
- honey
- maple syrup
- light corn syrup
- garlic
- onions
- potatoes

Herbs, spices, and condiments

- salt and black pepper
- ground spices (cumin, coriander, cinnamon, ginger)
- paprika
- dried red pepper flakes
- dried herbs (basil, oregano, rosemary, sage, thyme, mixed herbs)
- dry mustard
- whole-grain mustard
- harissa
- Tabasco sauce
- Worcestershire sauce
- sweet chili sauce
- ketchup
- mayonnaise
- Thai fish sauce
- soy sauce (dark, light)
- bouillon cubes or concentrates (vegetable, chicken, beef)
- tomato paste
- vinegars (red wine, white wine, balsamic)

In the freezer

- frozen meat and fish
- frozen vegetables (peas, corn kernels, spinach)
- puff pastry
- breads (including tortilla wraps, pita bread)

In the refrigerator

- eggs
- butter
- milk
- plain yogurt
- cheese (American, cheddar, Swiss, Parmesan)
- fresh herbs (cilantro, parsley, chives, mint, basil)
- fresh chiles
- fresh ginger root
- lemons
- celery
- carrots
- scallions
- bacon
- chorizo

Learning to Cheat

There are things you can do to make life easier for yourself in the kitchen. For example, cook larger-than-needed portions and eat the same meal for two days in a row to avoid cooking every day. Or transform the remainder into a new meal with a little thought and some useful kitchen staples. For instance, if you have leftover ground beef and tomato sauce for pasta, add a few shakes of Tabasco sauce and a can of red kidney beans and serve a chili the next day.

You don't always have to follow a recipe. Having a few reliable fall-back ingredients should stop you from reaching for that delivery pizza menu. For example, bake a potato and fill it with canned tuna, tomato, and cheese or hot baked beans for a quick, filling, and nutritious meal. Or make a quick, simple tomato sauce, then add whatever you have in the refrigerator or cupboard (such as chopped ham, mushrooms, or a pinch of dried red pepper flakes) to liven it up and serve it with pasta. Or use leftover vegetables to make a hearty bowl of soup— sauté them gently, then fill up the pan with hot water and a bouillon cube and simmer until tender. Once tender, blend until smooth or ladle into bowls as a chunky soup. And remember, if you have eggs, you have a meal, whether it's a comforting hard-boiled egg with toast, a fried egg sandwich, or a simple cheese omelet.

Healthy Eating

There are many small choices you can make to eat for good health. For example, even if time is precious, don't skip breakfast. Make a fruit-filled smoothie to fuel your body for the coming day and check off a few of your five-a-day early on. Add some frozen vegetables to a pasta sauce to boost your veggie intake, and stir a can of corn kernels into the tuna sandwich you're making. Snack on fresh or dried fruits instead of cookies or potato chips. To pad out a meal, use cans of rinsed, drained beans. Choose whole-wheat pasta and brown rice. Also, use a wide variety of fresh fruits and vegetables, meats, and fish to keep your diet rich in a range of nutrients.

Store fresh fruit and vegetables correctly and eat them as soon as possible after purchasing to maximize the amount of nutrients you get from them. Vary cooking methods to include poaching, broiling, or baking. Avoid frying to reduce your fat intake, and buy leaner cuts of meat. If only Chinese or pizza will do, try making your own. It will be lower in fat and salt and taste better than "the real thing." Store-bought sauces often have simple recipes on the back of the jar, and you can buy decent prepared pizza crusts or mixes if you don't feel like making your own. Make it healthy by adding a colorful array of vegetable toppings.

Hygiene in the Kitchen

Use common sense and follow a few simple guidelines to avoid food poisoning. Be sure your refrigerator works well and that the temperature is correct (you can buy an inexpensive special refrigerator thermometer). Pack away chilled and frozen goods as soon as you get home from shopping. Rotate the contents of the refrigerator so that foods closest to their expiration dates are used up first.

Store raw meat and fish on the bottom shelf of the refrigerator, away from other foods, and keep vegetables in the vegetable drawer (which is designed for this use). Use airtight containers for storing leftovers, or cover them with plastic wrap.

Add refrigerator cleaning to any cleaning rota you have in your house or apartment—it may look clean, but a refrigerator can be the ideal place for lurking bacteria to multiply. The same can be said for the kitchen itself and countertop surfaces. Empty waste cans, clean the oven, sweep the floor, and wipe countertops to keep the kitchen clean and tidy and a place in which you will enjoy preparing food.

Have Fun!

Student life is supposed to be fun, and there is no need for shopping, preparation, and cooking to become a chore. Invite your friends around to help you prepare and enjoy some meals and you'll have friends for life—as well as many return invitations. Vary recipes as much as possible and be adventurous. Cooking could become a passion! Experiment, have fun in the kitchen, enjoy some great home-cooked meals, and hone a few skills—then take these skills home to impress your family during the school breaks!

Twelve Ways with Poultry

Protein-packed and full of flavor.

Creamy Chicken and Mushroom Soup 44

Chicken and Egg Sandwich Filler 60

Thai Broiled Chicken Sandwich 68

Citrus Chicken Salad 80

Sage and Lemon Stir-Fried Turkey 98

Lime and Ginger Chicken Bowl 112

Soy Chicken and Rice Noodles 146

Jalepeño Turkey Burgers 162

Bacon-Wrapped Pesto Chicken 192

Smoked Bacon and Chicken Packages 198

Turkey Tikka Skewers 204

Green Curry Noodle Soup 218

Twelve Ways with Bacon and Sausage

Thought these fried stalwarts were just for morning-after breakfast? Think again!

2 Sausage and Cheese Baked Beans 34

1 Bacon and Egg Baguettes 36

2 Barbecue Bacon Burger and Cheesy Fries 56

3 Sausage and Cheese Rolls 70

2 Spicy Chorizo and Tomato Pasta 104

1 Warm Bacon, Tomato, and Lima Bean Salad 110

1 Mexican Hot Dogs 128

3 Honey-Mustard Sausages with Potato Wedges 142

3 Lazy Bacon, Pea, and Zucchini Risotto 150

3 Stove-Top Chorizo Pizza 160

3 Chorizo and Bean Stew 172

3 One-Pan Roasted Sausages 212

Brain Boosters

Get the gray matter working with these omega-rich delights.

Smoked Salmon and Cream Cheese Bagel 42

Smoked Salmon and Chive Mayonnaise 64

Herbed Pan-Fried Salmon 76

Flaked Mackerel and Green Pepper Couscous 86

Sweet Chili Salmon Fish Cakes 92

Sardine and Three Bean Salad 102

Beet, Mackerel, and Goat Cheese Lentils 114

Warm Sardine, Bean, and Potato Salad 116

Lemon Salmon Nuggets 122

Teriyaki Salmon Noodles 180

Flaked Mackerel Salad with Lemon Dressing 202

Sardine and Potato Salad 226

Vegetable Delights

The easy way to your 5-a-day—your mother will be so proud.

Leek and Mushroom Pastry Pockets 40

Chili Corn Fritters 46

Mustard and Onion Tartlets 50

Vegetable Pasta Bowl 82

Healthy Green Bean and Broccoli Salad 96

Red Cabbage and Beet Lentils 108

Steamed Bulgur with Broiled Vegetables 138

Green Pepper and Mushroom Stroganoff 190

Margherita Tart 206

Roasted Red Peppers with Mozzarella and Couscous 220

Gingery Broiled Tofu with Noodles 222

Vegetable Curry with Rice 224

One-Dish Wonders

One dish = less dish washing. Simple.

French Onion Soup with
Cheesy Croutons 52

Sizzling Beef and Broccoli
Stir-Fry 78

Indian-Inspired Beef and
Sweet Potato with Spinach 84

Red Pepper, Kidney Bean,
and Spinach Stew 90

Spiced Vegetable and
Chickpea Soup 94

Quick Garlicky Tomato
Lentils 132

Creamy Fish Casserole 136

Chunky Spiced Bean Soup 140

Creamy Curried Shrimp 210

Frozen Fruit Pie 252

Fresh Fruit Salad 268

Raisin Sheet Cake 276

Cheap Eats

Can't face another frozen TV dinner? Salvation is here.

Apricot and Prune Granola 24

Corned Beef Hash 48

Cauliflower and Cheese Gratin 54

Broiled Harissa Lamb with Pita 88

Tuna and Olive Pasta 130

Potato, Cauliflower, and Spinach Curry 148

Lemon Butter Fried Fish 156

Tomato and Basil Soup 182

Barbecue Pork Cutlets with Corn and Rice 208

Vanilla and Raspberry Cupcakes 236

Chewy Oat and Raisin Bars 248

Chocolate Buttermilk Pancakes 254

Pasta, Noodles, and Rice

Filling, tasty, and great for feeding a crowd.

Tuna and Chive Rice Salad 58

Pasta Casserole with Blue Cheese and Walnuts 100

Carrot and Broccoli Vegetable Stir-Fry 106

Spaghetti and Meatballs with Spicy Tomato Sauce 120

Mushroom and Egg-Fried Rice 134

Pasta with Chile and Anchovies 152

Tuna Gnocchi Casserole 154

Vegetable Noodle Salad 164

Spicy Pea Pasta 166

Spaghetti with Garlic and Black Pepper 170

Poor Man's Pesto with Penne 196

Creamy Mushroom and Chive Risotto 214

Hangover Helpers

For days when a little extra help is needed ...

Honeyed Granola Pancakes 26

Blueberry and Maple
Smoothie 28

Spicy Peanut and
Beef Wrap 118

Cheese and Onion
Potato Waffles 144

Sweet-and-Sour Pork 168

Beef and Onion Wraps 174

Mexican Chili Hamburger 184

Spiced Lamb Kebab
with Couscous 186

Breaded Fish with Peas 216

Chocolate Orange
Cheesecake 240

Stewed Rhubarb
with Custard 250

Lemon Popping Candy
Cupcakes 262

QuickCook

Breakfast, Brunch, and Lunch

Recipes listed by cooking time

3O

2O

10

 **Apricot and Prune Granola**

Serves 4

½ cup whole hazelnuts
¾ cup rolled oats
2 cups Bran Flakes, All-Bran,
  or similar bran-base
  breakfast cereal
2 tablespoons sunflower
  or mixed seeds (optional)
½ cup sliced dried apricots
5 dried prunes, chopped

To serve

milk and honey
sliced banana or apple (optional)

- Place the hazelnuts in a small, dry skillet and heat gently for 4–5 minutes, shaking the skillet occasionally, until lightly toasted. Transfer into the bowl of a mortar, crush lightly with a pestle, and set aside to cool.

- Meanwhile, combine the oats, bran cereal, seeds, and dried fruits. Add the toasted hazelnuts, then divide among 4 bowls and serve immediately with milk and honey and sliced banana or apple, if desired. Alternatively, double the recipe and store for up to a week in an airtight container.

 2 Oatmeal with Apricots and Prunes Place ¾ cup sliced dried apricots and 10 sliced prunes in a small saucepan with ½ cup apple juice, ¼ teaspoon ground cinnamon, and 2 tablespoons honey. Simmer gently for 8–10 minutes, until the fruit is tender and syrupy. Set aside to cool slightly. Meanwhile, place 1⅔ cups rolled oats in a medium saucepan with 3¾ cups milk and a pinch of salt. Place over medium heat and bring to a boil, stirring frequently. Reduce the heat and simmer gently for 12–15 minutes, until the oats are cooked and the oatmeal is creamy. Spoon into bowls and serve topped with the syrupy fruit.

 3 Swiss-Style Muesli with Apricots, Prunes, and Yogurt In a bowl, combine 4 cups of your preferred muesli with 1¼ cups apple juice, 1 cup plain yogurt, 1 cup milk, 2 tablespoons honey, ⅓ cup chopped dried apricots, and 5 chopped prunes. Cover and set aside for at least 25 minutes or, alternatively, cover and refrigerate overnight for the following morning. Serve with slices of fresh banana or apple.

STU-BREA-SAP

Honeyed Granola Pancakes

Serves 4

1¼ cups all-purpose flour

2 teaspoons baking powder

2 eggs

1 cup plus 2 tablespoons milk

3 tablespoons honey

1⅔ cups crunchy, granola-style cereal, lightly crushed

4 tablespoons butter

To serve

honey

Greek yogurt (optional)

- Sift the flour and baking powder together into a large bowl, then make a well in the center of the mixture. Whisk together the eggs, milk, and honey and pour into the well. Whisk the wet ingredients in the well as you gradually incorporate the flour into the mixture. Stir in the granola.

- Melt a pat of butter in a large nonstick skillet and pour small amounts of the batter into the skillet to form small, thick pancakes that are about 3¼ inches in diameter. Cook over medium-low heat for 2–3 minutes, until bubbles start to appear on the surface of the pancakes. Flip over and cook the other side for another minute, until golden. Repeat with the remaining batter until you have made all the pancakes. (This quantity of batter should yield about 16 pancakes.)

- Arrange the pancakes on warm serving plates and serve immediately with a drizzle of honey and a dollop of Greek yogurt, if desired.

 Honeyed Granola Yogurt

Spoon 1 tablespoon honey into the bottom of 4 glasses. Divide 1⅔ cups plain or Greek yogurt among the glasses and top each one with 2–3 tablespoons of granola. Serve immediately.

Great Granola

Melt ¼ cup honey with 3 tablespoons butter in a large saucepan and stir in 2¼ cups rolled oats, ½ cup chopped nuts, ⅓ cup mixed or sunflower seeds, and ½ teaspoon ground cinnamon or ginger (optional). Transfer evenly onto a large baking sheet and bake in a preheated oven, at 325°F, for 15–20 minutes, until pale golden, turning once. Remove from the oven and let cool slightly, then stir in ½ cup raisins. Serve with milk or yogurt. Store in an airtight container for about 1 week.

 # Blueberry and Maple Smoothie

Serves 6

6 bananas

3 small handfuls of blueberries

2¼ cups fruit-and-nut muesli

2¼ cups plain or fruit yogurt

3 cups milk

3–6 tablespoons maple syrup
  or honey

- Place 2 bananas and a small handful of blueberries in the pitcher of a blender and add ¾ cup muesli, ¾ cup yogurt, 1 cup milk, and 1–2 tablespoons honey or maple syrup. Blend until smooth but thick, then pour into 2 tall glasses to serve. Repeat twice to make 4 more smoothies.

- Alternatively, if you do not own a blender, pour the muesli into 6 bowls, spoon the yogurt over the cereal, and top with the sliced banana. Sprinkle with the blueberries, drizzle with the honey or maple syrup, and serve with spoons as a filling breakfast.

 ### Blueberry Maple Pancakes

In a bowl, mix 1¾ cups sifted all-purpose flour with 1 tablespoon baking powder and make a slight dip in the center. Add 1 lightly beaten, extra-large egg, 1 tablespoon melted butter, and 1¼ cups buttermilk and whisk until smooth and thick. Stir in ½ cup fresh or frozen blueberries. Melt 2 tablespoons butter in a nonstick skillet and pour 3–4 large tablespoons of the batter into the skillet. Cook gently for 2–3 minutes, until bubbles begin to appear on the surface of the pancakes, then carefully flip them over and cook for another minute, until golden. Remove and keep warm while you repeat the process to use up the remaining batter (this quantity yields about 12 pancakes). To serve, top with slices or crispy bacon, if desired, and drizzle with warm maple syrup.

 ### Blueberry Maple Breakfast Muffin

In a large bowl, mix 1⅔ cups all-purpose flour, ⅓ cup granulated sugar, 2 teaspoons baking powder, ½ teaspoon vanilla extract (optional), and ¼ cup muesli. Whisk ⅓ cup vegetable oil with 1 cup plain yogurt and 2 eggs and pour into the bowl with ⅔ cup blueberries. Stir until barely combined. Divide among the cups of a greased or paper cup-lined, 12-cup muffin pan and bake in a preheated oven, at 350°F, for 18–20 minutes. Serve warm, drizzled with maple syrup.

30 Banana and Bran Muffins

Serves 4

1 cup banana chips, crushed

1⅔ cups all-purpose flour

2 teaspoons baking powder

½ teaspoon ground cinnamon (optional)

¼ cup firmly packed dark brown or granulated sugar

⅔ cup wheat bran or crushed All-Bran cereal

2 eggs

4 tablespoons butter, melted

½ cup buttermilk

1 ripe banana, mashed

- Place the banana chips in a large bowl with the remaining dry ingredients. Whisk together all the remaining ingredients in a small bowl.

- Pour the wet ingredients into the dry ingredients and stir until barely combined. Divide the batter among the cups of a greased or paper cup-lined, 12-cup muffin pan and bake in a preheated oven, at 350°F, for 18–22 minutes, until risen and firm to the touch. Transfer to wire racks to cool slightly and serve warm.

 **Banana-Topped Toast** Toast and butter 4 thick slices of whole-wheat or multigrain bread. In a bowl, mash 2 ripe bananas with ¼ teaspoon ground cinnamon and 2 teaspoons honey. Spread this mixture thickly over the buttered toast and top each one with a heapingt teaspoon of your preferred fruit preserves. Serve with glasses of orange juice and a small container of yogurt for a healthy, balanced breakfast.

 Baked Banana and Bran Oatmeal Wrap 4 bananas in aluminum foil and bake in a preheated oven, at 350°F, for 10–15 minutes, until the skins are blackened and the flesh has softened. Meanwhile, put 1⅓ cups rolled oats in a medium saucepan with 1 cup wheat bran, 3¾ cups milk, a pinch of salt, and ½ teaspoon ground cinnamon (optional). Put over medium heat and bring to a boil, stirring frequently. Reduce the heat and simmer gently for 12–15 minutes, stirring frequently, until the oats are cooked and the oatmeal is creamy. Scrape the flesh of the bananas into the pan and stir into the hot oatmeal. Spoon into bowls and sprinkle with a teaspoon of brown sugar to serve, if desired.

Quick Ham and Eggs Benedict

Serves 2

2 teaspoons white wine
or cider vinegar

4 eggs

1 tablespoon butter

½ (1¼ oz) envelope Hollandaise
sauce mix

⅔ cup milk

2 English muffins, split

4 oz wafer-thin ham

black pepper

- Bring a large saucepan of water to a gentle simmer and add the vinegar. Stir the water with a large spoon to create a swirl and carefully crack an egg into the water, followed by a second egg. Cook for 3 minutes, then remove with a slotted spoon and keep warm. Repeat with the remaining eggs.

- Meanwhile, melt the butter in a small saucepan and stir in the Hollandaise mix. Slowly pour in the milk, stirring to prevent lumps from forming. Bring to a boil, then reduce the heat and simmer gently for 1–2 minutes. (Alternatively, make the Hollandaise sauce according to the package directions.)

- Lightly toast the muffins and arrange on serving plates. Top each muffin half with some ham. Place 1 poached egg on top of each muffin half and spoon some sauce over the top. Season with black pepper and serve immediately.

 Quick Ham and Egg Tortilla Melt 2 tablespoons butter in a skillet and cook 3 thinly sliced scallions over medium heat for 3–4 minutes, until softened. Meanwhile, beat 5 eggs with a pinch each of salt and black pepper. Add ½ cup drained and sliced roasted red pepper, 8 oz chopped ham, and 1 tablespoon chopped chives (optional). Pour into the skillet and cook gently for 4–5 minutes, until almost set. Crumble 4 oz goat cheese or feta over the top and cook under a preheated medium-high broiler for 2–3 minutes, until golden. Cool slightly, then serve in wedges.

 Quick Baked Ham and Egg Heat 2 tablespoons butter in a large skillet and cook 3 thinly sliced scallions over medium heat for 3–4 minutes, until softened. Add 4 cups washed spinach leaves and stir for 1–2 minutes, until wilted. Remove from the heat and mix with 8 oz chopped ham and 1 tablespoon chopped chives or parsley (optional). Scrape the mixture into a buttered, shallow ovenproof dish, then carefully crack 4 eggs over the top. Drizzle ½ cup heavy cream over the eggs, sprinkle with grated Parmesan cheese, and bake in a preheated oven, at 400°F, for 15–20 minutes, until the eggs are just set but still creamy. Remove from the oven and serve with plenty of crusty bread. (Alternatively, divide the mixture between 2 individual dishes or shallow ramekins and cook for 10–15 minutes, until just set but still creamy.)

Sausage and Cheese Baked Beans

Serves 2

4 herb-flavored link sausages

1 tablespoon vegetable oil

1 garlic clove, crushed

1 teaspoon paprika (optional)

1 teaspoon onion powder
  (optional)

1 (15 oz) can navy beans,
  rinsed and drained

1⅓ cups tomato puree
  or tomato sauce

1 teaspoon Worcestershire sauce

1 teaspoon packed brown sugar
  or molasses

2–4 slices of your preferred bread

butter, for spreading

1 cup shredded cheddar cheese

- Arrange the sausages on the rack of an aluminum foil-lined broiler pan and slide the pan under a broiler preheated to a medium setting. Broil the sausages for about 15 minutes, turning occasionally, until cooked through and golden. Remove and keep warm.

- While the sausages are cooking, heat the oil in a saucepan and cook the garlic gently for 1 minute before adding the paprika. Cook for another minute, then add the onion powder (if using), beans, tomato puree or sauce, Worcestershire sauce, and sugar or molasses. Simmer gently for about 15 minutes, until the beans are soft and the sauce has thickened slightly.

- Toward the end of the cooking time for the beans and sausages, toast and butter the slices of bread.

- Slice the sausages thickly, then combine with the beans. According to preference, either stir the cheese into the mixture, then spoon it onto the buttered toast, or spoon the beans-and-sausage mixture onto the buttered toast and sprinkle with the shredded cheese.

 Sausage and Scrambled Eggs

Beat 4 eggs with 3 tablespoons milk and a pinch of salt and black pepper. Melt 2 tablespoons butter in a nonstick saucepan. Pour in the eggs. When they begin to set, stir gently over low heat for 3–4 minutes, until just set. Stir in 4 sliced frankfurters or cooked sausages and heat gently until the eggs are lightly set but creamy and the sausages are heated through. Spoon onto hot buttered toast to serve.

 One-Pan Sausage and Eggs

Heat 2 tablespoons vegetable oil in a large nonstick skillet and add 4 thin pork sausages. Cook over medium heat, turning occasionally, for 10–12 minutes, until cooked through. Remove from the skillet and set aside. Add 4 slices of bacon and cook over medium heat for 2–3 minutes on each side, until crisp and golden. Remove from the skillet and set aside. Add 3 cups sliced mushrooms to the skillet and cook over medium heat for 4–5 minutes, turning occasionally, until softened. Return the meats to the skillet and arrange so that you have equal amounts on each side of the skillet. Crack 1 egg into each half of the skillet and cook gently for 3–5 minutes, depending on how well done you like your eggs. Use a spatula to lift the cooked breakfasts onto 2 plates and serve with plenty of buttered toast.

STU-BREA-MUX

1⏲ Bacon and Egg Baguettes

Serves 2

2 tablespoons butter or margarine

3 eggs

1 tablespoon chopped chives

6 bacon slices

2 individual sandwich baguettes

your preferred condiment
(such as ketchup, barbecue
sauce, or mayonnaise)

2 small handfuls of arugula or
baby spinach (optional)

salt and black pepper

- Melt the butter gently in a large skillet while you beat the eggs with the chives and seasoning in a small bowl. Pour the egg mixture into the skillet and swirl to cover the bottom of the skillet. Cook over medium heat for 2–3 minutes, until the bottom is golden. Flip over and cook for another 2 minutes or until the egg is set and both sides are golden. Remove from the skillet, cool slightly, then cut into slices.

- While the eggs are cooking, arrange the bacon on the rack of an aluminum foil-lined broiler pan and cook under a broiler preheated to a medium setting for 4–5 minutes, until crisp.

- Slice open the baguettes and spread with your preferred condiment before topping with the egg, bacon, and arugula or spinach leaves, if using. Serve immediately.

2⏲ Bacon, Egg, and Cheese Panini

Heat 1 tablespoon vegetable oil in a skillet and cook 6 bacon slices over medium heat for 4–5 minutes, turning once, until crisp. (Alternatively, arrange the bacon on the rack of an aluminum foil-lined broiler pan and cook under a broiler preheated to a medium setting for the same amount of time.) Remove the bacon and drain on paper towels. Split open 2 large bread rolls and spread each roll with 2 teaspoons whole-grain mustard or your preferred condiment. Fill the rolls with the crispy bacon and top each with 2 slices American or cheddar cheese, then sprinkle

½ thinly sliced red onion over the cheese, if desired, and close. Heat a dry skillet and place the rolls in the skillet. Weigh them down by resting a saucepan on top and toast over medium-low heat for 2–3 minutes, until crisp and golden. Flip over and toast the other side for another 2–3 minutes, until the rolls are toasted and the cheese is melting. Meanwhile, crack 2 eggs into the skillet, adding a little butter or oil, if necessary, and cook over medium heat for 3–4 minutes, until the eggs are cooked to your liking. Remove the paninis from the skillet and serve each one topped with a fried egg.

3⏲ Bacon and Cheese Spanish Omelet

Heat 1 tablespoon oil in a skillet with a pat of butter and cook 4 chopped bacon slices over medium heat for 5–6 minutes. Add 1 sliced onion and cook for 7–8 minutes, until softened. Meanwhile, beat 3 eggs with 1 tablespoon chopped chives and a pinch each of salt and black pepper. Reduce the heat, stir the eggs into the skillet, and cook gently for 4–5 minutes, until almost set. Sprinkle with 1 cup shredded American, Swiss, or cheddar cheese and transfer to a medium broiler for 4–5 minutes, until the egg has set and the topping is golden. Cut into wedges to serve.

STU-BREA-QEE

10 Spicy Brunch Quesadillas

Serves 2

1 cup refried beans

4 plain tortilla wraps

1 small avocado, pitted, peeled, and diced

2 tomatoes, diced

4 oz sliced mozzarella or 1 cup shredded cheddar cheese

shredded iceberg lettuce (optional), to serve

- Spread the refried beans over 2 of the tortillas, then sprinkle with the avocado and tomato. Sprinkle with the mozzarella or shredded cheddar, then top each with another tortilla.

- Heat a large skillet and toast 1 of the quesadillas over medium heat for 1–2 minutes before flipping it over to toast the other side. Repeat with the second quesadilla. Serve in wedges with shredded lettuce, if desired.

2 Spicy Brunch Burritos

Heat 2 tablespoons vegetable oil in a skillet and cook 1 sliced onion over medium heat for 6–7 minutes, until softened. Add 3 cups sliced mushrooms and cook for 4–5 minutes. Stir in ⅔ cup drained canned corn kernels and 4 sliced frankfurters and heat gently for 1–2 minutes, until hot. (Alternatively, for a vegetarian dish, use a 1 cup rinsed and drained canned chickpeas in place of the sausages.) Spoon the filling onto 4 plain tortilla wraps and top each with 1 tablespoon spicy tomato salsa and a few drops of Tabasco sauce for extra heat. Sprinkle with 3 oz diced or grated mozzarella and roll up each tortilla. Serve hot.

3 Spicy Brunch Enchiladas

In a medium bowl, combine ⅔ cup drained canned corn kernels with 2 thinly sliced scallions, 1 cup rinsed and drained canned chickpeas, ½ (4 oz) ball of mozzarella, diced, and ½ (12–13 oz) jar of Mexican cooking sauce (such as enchilada or fajita sauce) or ½ (14½ oz) can diced tomatoes. Spoon the filling into 4 plain tortilla wraps, then roll tightly and arrange snugly in an ovenproof dish. Pour over another ½ (12–13 oz) jar of the sauce or ½ (14½ oz) can diced tomatoes and sprinkle with the remaining ½ (4 oz) ball mozzarella, diced. Cook in a preheated oven, at 400°F, for 15–20 minutes, until bubbling and golden. Serve hot with a dollop of sour cream, if desired.

Leek and Mushroom Pastry Pockets

Serves 4

4 tablespoons butter

2 leeks, trimmed and sliced

7 cups (1 lb) mushrooms, halved
   (or quartered, if large)

1 cup cream cheese

1 teaspoon dried tarragon or
   1 tablespoon chopped tarragon

1 (1 lb) package ready-to-bake
   puff pastry

flour, for dusting

1 medium egg, lightly beaten

salt and black pepper

- Melt the butter in a large skillet and cook the leeks over medium heat for 3 minutes, stirring occasionally, until they begin to soften. Add the mushrooms and continue to cook for another 4–5 minutes, until tender and lightly golden, then stir in the cream cheese and tarragon.

- Meanwhile, roll out the pastry on a lightly floured surface and cut into four 8 inch circles. Brush a ½ inch border with a little beaten egg.

- Season the leek and mushrooms with a pinch each of salt and black pepper and divide the mixture among the 4 circles. Bring up 2 sides of the pastry to encase the filling, crimping the pastry together with your fingers to seal the edges.

- Arrange the filled pastry pockets on a baking sheet, brush with the remaining beaten egg, and cook in a preheated oven, at 400°F, for about 18 minutes, until puffed up and golden. Serve warm.

 Buttery Leek and Mushrooms on Toast Melt 6 tablespoons butter in a skillet and add 2 sliced leeks and 3 cups sliced mushrooms with 1 teaspoon dried tarragon or 1 tablespoon fresh tarragon, if desired, and a pinch of salt and black pepper. Cook over medium heat for 8–10 minutes, stirring occasionally, until soft and golden. Meanwhile, toast 4 thick slices of bread, spread each with 1 tablespoon cream cheese, and arrange on plates. Spoon the buttery leeks and mushrooms over the toast to serve.

 Leek and Mushroom Frittata Melt 4 tablespoons butter in a large skillet and cook the leeks and mushrooms as above. Add 1 (14½ oz) canned whole new potatoes, drained and sliced, to the skillet for the final minute to heat. Meanwhile, beat 5 eggs with a pinch each of salt and black pepper and 1 teaspoon dried tarragon (optional). Pour the eggs into the skillet, stir to combine, and cook over medium-low heat for 5–6 minutes, until almost set. Sprinkle with 3 tablespoons finely grated Parmesan cheese and cook under a broiler preheated to a medium setting for 3–4 minutes, until the frittata is set. Serve in wedges, with salad.

1️⃣ Smoked Salmon and Cream Cheese Bagel

Serves 4

4 plain or onion bagels, split
⅓ cup plain or chive and onion
cream cheese
¼ cucumber, sliced (optional)
4 oz sliced smoked salmon
1 tablespoon chopped chives
(optional)
4 teaspoons lemon juice
black pepper

- Arrange the bagels, cut side up, on a baking sheet and toast under a broiler preheated to a medium setting for 2–3 minutes, until golden.

- Spread the bottom halves if the bagels with the cream cheese and top with the cucumber, if using. Sprinkle the smoked salmon over the cucumber and sprinkle with the chopped chives, if using. Drizzle with lemon juice and season generously with black pepper.

- Top with the lid and serve.

Smoked Salmon Scrambled Eggs

Melt 4 tablespoons butter in a large nonstick saucepan and gently cook 2 finely chopped shallots for 7–8 minutes, until really soft. Beat 8 eggs in a bowl with ⅓ cup milk, ¼ cup cream cheese, and a generous pinch of black pepper. Pour the mixture into the saucepan and stir gently over low heat for 5–6 minutes, until the eggs are lightly set but still creamy. Meanwhile, toast 4 bagels as above, or 8 small slices of whole-grain bread. Spread with

butter and arrange on serving plates. Spoon the scrambled egg onto the bagels or toast and sprinkle with 4 oz sliced smoked salmon. Garnish with 1 tablespoon chopped chives, if desired, and season with black pepper.

Smoked Salmon and Herb Tart

Unroll 1 sheet ready-to-bake puff pastry sheet and use it to line a 9 inch tart pan. Sprinkle 4 oz sliced smoked salmon over the bottom. In a bowl, lightly beat 4 eggs, 2 tablespoons cream cheese, 1 tablespoon chopped chives, a pinch of salt, and a generous pinch of pepper. Pour the mixture over the salmon and cook in a preheated oven, at 400°C, for 20–25 minutes, until golden. Slice into wedges and serve hot or cold.

Creamy Chicken and Mushroom Soup

Serves 4

2 tablespoons olive or
   vegetable oil
1 onion, chopped
1 celery stick or leek, chopped
6 cups chopped mushrooms
3 cups hot chicken
   or vegetable stock
2 cups shredded cooked chicken
¼ cup light or heavy cream
salt and black pepper
crusty bread, to serve (optional)

- Heat the oil in a large saucepan and cook the onion and celery or leek over medium heat for 7–8 minutes, until softened. Stir in the mushrooms and cook for another 3–4 minutes, until softened, then pour in the hot stock, bring to a boil, and simmer gently for 5–6 minutes, until all the vegetables are tender.

- Remove from the heat and use a handheld immersion blender or food processor to blend until almost smooth. (Alternatively, if you don't have a blender, push the soup through strainer, or serve as chunky soup.) Stir in the shredded chicken and cream, then season to taste and stir over the heat for 1 final minute, until hot but not boiling. Ladle into mugs or bowls and serve with crusty bread, if desired.

Creamy Broiled Mushrooms

Brush 12 large flat mushrooms with oil and arrange on an aluminum foil-lined baking sheet. Sprinkle with salt and black pepper and cook under a broiler preheated to a medium setting for 4–5 minutes, until tender. Remove from the broiler, top each one with a tablespoon of garlic-and-herb cream cheese, and return to the broiler for another 1–2 minutes, until the cheese is melting. Serve on toasted bread or with mixed salad greens.

Creamy Chicken and Mushroom Pie

Melt a pat of butter in a skillet and cook 2 trimmed and sliced leeks and 6 cups halved or quartered mushrooms for 7–8 minutes, stirring occasionally, until softened, then transfer to a bowl with ½ cup store-bought cheese, carbonara, or white sauce, 2 cups shredded, cooked chicken, and ⅓ cup garlic-and-herb cream cheese. Mix to combine, then spoon into a medium ovenproof dish. Spoon 2 cups cold mashed potatoes on top of the chicken-and-mushroom mixture and sprinkle with 1 cup shredded cheddar cheese. Bake in a preheated oven, at 400°F, for 15–18 minutes, until crisp and golden.

2⏱ Chili Corn Fritters

Serves 4

⅓ cup all-purpose flour

2 eggs

2 tablespoons sweet chili sauce,
  plus extra for dipping

1 (15 oz) can corn kernels, drained

4 tablespoons butter

salt and black pepper

- Place the flour in a bowl and add the eggs and sweet chili sauce. Whisk to combine, then gently stir the corn kernels and seasoning into the mixture.

- Melt about one-third of the butter in a skillet and drop 5–6 tablespoons of the batter into the skillet in separate puddles, flattening each one gently. Cook gently over medium-low heat for about 3 minutes, until the bottoms of the fritters are golden, then flip over each one carefully and cook the other side for 2–3 minutes.

- Repeat with the remaining butter and batter until you have used up all the batter and made about 16 fritters.

- Serve hot with extra chili sauce for dipping, if desired.

1⏱ Chili Corn Cheese Muffins

Split 4 whole-wheat English muffins in half and toast in a toaster until lightly golden. Meanwhile, place 1⅓ cups shredded cheddar or Monterey jack cheese in a bowl with 3 tablespoons sweet chili sauce, 2 tablespoons chopped chives (optional), and 1 (8¼ oz) can drained corn kernels. Season with salt and black pepper and mix to combine. Spread thickly over the muffins, arrange on a lined baking sheet, and cook under a broiler preheated to a medium setting for 3–4 minutes, until golden and melted. Serve hot with extra sweet chili sauce.

3⏱ Chili Corn Muffins

Sift 1¾ cups all-purpose flour into a bowl with 1 teaspoon baking powder and ½ teaspoon each of salt and black pepper. Rub 4 tablespoons butter into the flour until the mixture resembles bread crumbs, then stir in 1 tablespoon chopped chives (optional). Set aside. In a small bowl, whisk 1 egg with 2 tablespoons sweet chile sauce, ½ cup milk, ⅓ cup vegetable oil, and ⅔ cup drained canned corn kernels. Pour the wet ingredients into the dry ingredients and stir until barely combined. Divide the batter among the cups of a greased or paper cup-lined, 12-cup muffin pan, sprinkle with ½ cup cheddar or Monterey jack cheese, and bake in a preheated oven, at 400°F, for 18–20 minutes, until risen and golden.

 # Corned Beef Hash

Serves 4

6 Yukong gold or russet potatoes, peeled and diced

3 tablespoons of oil

1 large onion, chopped

2 garlic cloves, chopped

1 (12 oz) can corned beef, chopped or crumbled

To serve

4 fried eggs

2 tablespoons chopped parsley (optional)

your preferred condiment (such as ketchup or barbecue sauce; optional)

- Cook the potatoes in a large saucepan of boiling water for about 10 minutes, until just tender. Drain well.

- Meanwhile, heat 2 tablespoons of the oil in a large nonstick skillet and cook the onion and garlic over medium-low heat for 7–8 minutes, until softened.

- Add the remaining oil to the pan with the corned beef and drained potatoes and mix well. Continue to cook for about 15 minutes, turning occasionally—but not too often—until crispy and golden.

- Spoon onto 4 warm plates and top with the fried eggs and parsley, if using. Serve immediately with a choice of ketchup or barbecue sauce, if desired.

 ### Corned Beef and Onion Bagel

Heat 2 tablespoons vegetable oil in a skillet and add 1 thinly sliced onion. Cook gently for 8–10 minutes, until soft and golden. Meanwhile, toast 4 split plain or onion bagels. Mix together 1 tablespoon each of mayonnaise and whole-grain mustard and spread over the bottom half of each toasted bagel. Slice the corned beef from 1 (12 oz) can and arrange over the mustard mayonnaise. Place on serving plates and serve topped with the onions and toasted lid.

 ### Corned Beef Fritters

In a bowl, whisk 2 eggs with ¾ cup all-purpose flour, 1¾ teaspoons baking powder, and ½ cup milk until smooth. Add 2 tablespoons chopped parsley (optional), the chopped corned beef from 1 (12 oz) can, 1 cup diced, cooked potatoes, and 2 finely chopped scallions and mix to combine. Heat 2 tablespoons vegetable oil in a large nonstick skillet and drop heaping tablespoons of the mixture into the skillet, flattening them slightly with the back of the spoon into 4 inch fritters. Cook over medium heat for about 2 minutes on each side, until golden, then drain on paper towels and repeat with the remaining mixture, adding extra oil to the skillet, if necessary, until you have made about 12 fritters. Serve hot with a choice of ketchup or barbecue sauce for dipping.

Mustard and Onion Tartlets

Serves 2

1 sheet ready-to-bake
puff pastry

2 tablespoons whole-grain
mustard

5 oz Brie or Camembert cheese,
sliced

1 tablespoon beaten egg or milk,
to brush

2 scallions or ½ small red onion,
finely sliced

½ teaspoon dried thyme
(optional)

salad green, to serve

· Cut the puff pastry in half to form 2 rectangles and place these on a baking sheet. Spread the mustard over the bottoms, leaving a ½ inch border, and top with the sliced Brie. Brush the border with the beaten egg or milk.

· Sprinkle with the scallion and thyme, if using, and bake in a preheated oven, at 400°F, for 12–15 minutes, until crisp and golden.

· Serve with salad greens.

Mustard and Onion Melts Slice 1 French bread into thick diagonal slices. Spread ½ teaspoon whole-grain mustard over each slice and top with ½ small red onion, thinly sliced. Top each piece with a slice of goat cheese and arrange on the rack of an aluminum foil-lined broiler pan. Cook under a broiler preheated to a medium-hot setting for 3–4 minutes or until the cheese is melting. Serve on top of salad greens drizzled with a French-style dressing.

Leek, Mustard, and Onion Tart Melt 4 tablespoons butter in a large skillet, then slice 3 trimmed leeks and 1 red onion and cook in the skillet over medium-low heat, stirring occasionally, for 8–10 minutes, until softened. Meanwhile, unroll a sheet of ready-to-bake puff pastry on a baking sheet and lightly score a ¾ inch border around the edge. Brush the border with a little beaten egg or milk. Mix together 2 tablespoons whole-grain mustard and 2 tablespoons cream cheese and spread over the bottom of the pastry, keeping within the border. Top with the softened leek-and-onion mixture, then cover with 5 oz sliced Brie or Camembert. Bake in a preheated oven, at 375°F, for 18–20 minutes, until crisp and golden and the cheese has melted.

30 French Onion Soup with Cheesy Croutons

Serves 2

4 tablespoons butter

3 large onions, halved and
thinly sliced

2 garlic cloves, coarsely chopped

1 tablespoon all-purpose flour

2 cups hot beef stock

1 teaspoon dried thyme or
2 teaspoons chopped thyme

1 individual sandwich baguette

1 cup shredded Swiss
or cheddar cheese

salt and black pepper

- Melt the butter in a large saucepan and cook the onions over medium heat for about 15 minutes, stirring occasionally, until soft and golden. Add the garlic and continue for another 5 minutes, until the onion is a deeper golden color. Stir in the flour for 1 minute.

- Stir in the beef stock and thyme, bring to a boil, and simmer gently for 8–10 minutes to let the flavors to develop. Season to taste.

- Meanwhile, slice the baguette and top with the shredded cheese. Cook under a broiler preheated to a medium-hot setting for 2–3 minutes, until the cheese is melting and golden.

- To serve, ladle the soup into 2 deep bowls and top with the cheesy croutons.

 **Open Grilled Brie Sandwich** Thickly slice 5 oz Brie or Camembert. Spread each of 2 slices of bread with 1 tablespoon onion chutney (optional) and top with the sliced cheese. Sprinkle with 1 finely sliced scallion, then top each one with a second slice of bread. Melt 2 tablespoons butter in a large skillet and add the sandwiches to the skillet. Toast over medium-high heat for 1–2 minutes on each side, until golden and crispy. Serve hot with salad greens.

 Egg-Topped Grilled Cheese Sandwich In a bowl, mix 1⅓ cups shredded cheddar or Swiss cheese with ½ red onion, finely sliced, 1 tablespoon whole-grain mustard, and 1 tablespoon crème fraîche. Spread this mixture over 2 thick slices of bread, then top each one with 2 oz thinly sliced ham. Top with a second slice of bread. Melt 2 tablespoons of butter in a large skillet and lay the sandwiches in the skillet. Cook over medium-low heat for 4–6 minutes, turning once, until golden. Remove from the skillet and keep warm while you add 1 tablespoon vegetable oil to the skillet and crack 2 eggs into the oil. Cook over medium heat for 3–5 minutes, depending on how well done you like your eggs, then remove with a spatula. Arrange the toasted sandwiches on serving plates with salad greens and top each one with a fried egg. Serve immediately with a drizzle of vinaigrette over the greens, if desired.

STU-BREA-ZIP

Cauliflower and Cheese Gratin

Serves 4

1 head of cauliflower,
  broken into large pieces
⅓ cup all-purpose flour
2 tablespoons butter,
  plus extra for greasing
1 teaspoon dry mustard (optional)
2 cups milk
2 cups shredded cheddar or
  American cheese
salt and black pepper

- Bring a large saucepan of lightly salted water to a boil and cook the cauliflower for 7–8 minutes, until just tender. Drain well.

- Meanwhile, place the flour, butter, and dry mustard, if using, in a medium saucepan with the milk. Slowly bring to a boil, stirring constantly, until smooth and thickened. Stir in 1 cup of the cheese and, once it has melted, season to taste.

- Transfer the cauliflower to a buttered ovenproof dish, pour the cheesy sauce over the vegetable, and sprinkle with the remaining cheese.

- Cook under a broiler preheated to a medium-hot setting for 3–4 minutes, until golden. (Alternatively, if you do not have a broiler, cook in a preheated oven, at 400°F, for 10–12 minutes, until bubbling and golden.)

 Creamy Cauliflower Coleslaw In a large bowl, mix ⅔ cup plain yogurt with 1 teaspoon mild mustard, 3 tablespoons mayonnaise, and 2 teaspoons vinegar, then season with a pinch each of salt and black pepper. Slice 1 small head of cauliflower thinly and scrape into the bowl with 2 peeled and shredded carrots. Mix really well to coat in the dressing, then serve with toasted pita breads.

 Potato and Cauliflower Soup Melt 2 tablespoons butter in a large saucepan with 1 tablespoon vegetable oil and cook 1 finely chopped onion and 2 large potatoes, peeled and diced, over medium heat for 8–10 minutes, until the onion is softened and lightly golden. Stir in 1 teaspoon cumin seeds and 1 small head of cauliflower that has been broken into florets, and continue to cook, stirring frequently for 3–4 minutes, until the cauliflower begins to soften slightly. Pour in 3¾ cups vegetable stock and bring to a boil. Reduce the heat, cover, and simmer gently for about 15 minutes, until the vegetables are really tender. Blend with a handheld blender until smooth or, if you do not own a blender, press through a strainer or colander. Ladle into bowls and serve topped with croutons.

Barbecue Bacon Burger and Cheesy Fries

Serves 2

8 oz ready-to-bake frozen
   French fries
2 tablespoons vegetable oil
4 bacon slices
8 oz ground beef
1 teaspoon dried oregano
½ red onion, very finely chopped
   (optional)
⅓ cup crumbled blue cheese
½ cup shredded cheddar cheese
salt and black pepper

To serve

barbecue sauce
large burger buns, split and
   toasted

- Arrange the French fries in a single layer on a large baking sheet and cook in a preheated oven, at 425°F, for 15–18 minutes, or according to the package directions, until crisp and golden.

- Meanwhile, heat the vegetable oil in a medium skillet and cook the bacon over medium heat for 4–5 minutes, until golden. Remove from the skillet and keep warm.

- While the bacon is cooking, mix the ground beef in a bowl with the oregano, onion, blue cheese, and a pinch each of salt and black pepper. Shape into 2 patties and cook in the skillet over medium heat for 5 minutes on each side, until cooked through but still juicy.

- Assemble the burgers in burger buns with the cooked bacon and a dollop of barbecue sauce, adding other fillings of your choice, if desired.

- Remove the fries from the oven, put into bowls, and sprinkle with the shredded cheese. Serve alongside the burgers.

Barbecue Bacon Bagel

Arrange 6 bacon slices on the rack of an aluminum foil-lined broiler pan and brush with 2 tablespoons barbecue marinade. Cook under a broiler preheated to a medium setting for 5–7 minutes, turning once, until cooked. Meanwhile, toast 2 plain or sesame bagels and arrange on serving plates. Top each bottom half with 2 tablespoons coleslaw, then lay the bacon slices on top. Finish with a green lettuce leaf and cover with the lid to serve.

Barbecue Pork Strips

Lay 6 pork belly slices in an ovenproof dish, then pour over ¼ cup barbecue marinade and rub it into the meat to coat it really well. Set aside to marinate for at least 15 minutes. Meanwhile, bring a large saucepan of lightly salted water to a boil. Rinse 1 cup instant long-grain rice under running water, then cook in a boiling water according to the package directions, until just tender, then drain. Arrange the pork belly

slices on the rack of an aluminum foil-lined broiler pan and cook under a preheated medium-hot broiler for 4–5 minutes on each side until sticky and cooked through but still juicy. Spoon the rice onto serving plates, top with the barbecue pork strips, and drizzle with any juices. Serve immediately with coleslaw, if desired.

 # Tuna and Chive Rice Salad

Serves 4

1½ cups instant long-grain rice

1 (15 oz) can red kidney beans, rinsed and drained

1 (8¾ oz) can corn kernels, rinsed and drained

4 scallions, finely sliced (optional)

1 (12 oz) can chunk light tuna in oil, drained and flaked

2 tablespoons chopped chives

salt

To serve

butterhead lettuce leaves

French-style vinaigrette

- Bring a large saucepan of lightly salted water to a boil, add the rice, then reduce to a simmer and cook the rice according to the package directions, until tender. Drain in a strainer and cool under running water. Drain well.

- Meanwhile, place the kidney beans in a large bowl and mix with the corn kernels, scallion, if using, tuna, and chives. Fold through the cold rice and spoon into bowls. Serve with the lettuce and French-style vinaigrette.

 ### Tuna and Chive Melts

Cut 2 sandwich baguettes in half horizontally. Mix 1 (5 oz) can drained and flaked chunk light tuna in oil with 1 seeded and chopped red bell pepper, ⅔ cup drained canned corn kernels, 2 sliced scallions, and 1 tablespoon chopped chives. Stir in ¼ cup salsa or mayonnaise. Spread thickly over the cut sides of the baguette and top with 1⅓ cups shredded cheddar cheese. Arrange on a baking sheet and cook under a broiler preheated to a medium setting for 4–5 minutes, until melted and golden. Serve with salad.

 ### Tuna, Chive, and Potato Gratin

Bring a large saucepan of lightly salted water to a boil and cook 4 red-skinned or white round potatoes, peeled and thinly sliced, for about 8 minutes, until just tender. Drain through a colander and transfer to a buttered, large ovenproof dish with 2 tablespoons chopped chives and 1 (12 oz) can drained and flaked chunk light tuna in oil. Meanwhile, heat 1¼ cups milk with ⅔ cup heavy cream, 1 finely chopped garlic clove, and a generous pinch each of salt and black pepper. Bring to the boiling point, then remove the mixture from the heat and pour it over the potato and tuna, shaking the dish to combine. Sprinkle with 1 cup shredded Muenster, American, or cheddar cheese of the top and bake in a preheated oven, at 425°F, for 15–20 minutes, until bubbling and golden.

 Chicken and Egg Sandwich Filler

Serves 2

3 eggs
2 tablespoons mayonnaise
½ teaspoon paprika (optional)
1 cup chopped, cooked
   chicken breast
salt and black pepper

To serve

whole-wheat sandwich bread
   or baked potatoes
small handful of alfalfa sprouts
   or cress

- Bring a small saucepan of water to a rolling boil and gently lower the eggs into the water. Cook for 8 minutes to hard boil the eggs. Remove from the water and sit in a bowl under running water until completely cold.

- Meanwhile, place the mayonnaise in a bowl with the paprika, if using, and a pinch each of salt and black pepper.

- Once cold, tap the eggs all over to break the shells. Peel away the shell and coarsely chop the hard-boiled eggs. Mash into the mayonnaise with the chopped chicken and either spread on bread to make sandwiches or spoon onto baked potatoes. Sprinkle with the sprouts or cress to serve.

 Tandoori Chicken Sandwich Filler

Place 3 tablespoons mayonnaise or plain yogurt in a bowl with 1 tablespoon tandoori paste, 1 teaspoon lemon juice, and 1 tablespoon chopped cilantro (optional) and stir well to combine. Add 2 cups cooked chunky chicken pieces (or use 8 oz roasted chicken with the skin removed, coarsely sliced) to the bowl and mix well to coat. Use this mixture to fill tortilla wraps with a handful of alfalfa sprouts and a teaspoon of mango chutney.

 Chicken and Onion Sandwich Filler

Heat 2 tablespoons vegetable oil in a large skillet and cook 2 sliced onions for 12–15 minutes, until soft and golden, stirring occasionally. Scrape into a bowl and set aside. Now increase the heat and add an extra tablespoon of oil. Add 8 oz thinly sliced skinless, boneless chicken breasts to the skillet and stir-fry for 7–8 minutes, until cooked through. Remove from the skillet and let rest for 2 minutes. Mix with the onion and use to fill sandwiches or as a topping for baked potato with mustardy or garlic mayonnaise and a handful of alfalfa sprouts.

Bean and Parsley Pâté

Serves 4

2 (15 oz) cans beans (such
   as navy or cannellini beans),
   rinsed and drained
3 tablespoons tomato paste
2 teaspoons lemon juice
½ teaspoon ground cumin
   (optional)
¼ cup plain or Greek yogurt
2 tablespoons chopped parsley,
   plus extra to garnish
salt and black pepper
hot toast, to serve

- Place the beans in a food processor with the tomato paste, lemon juice, and ground cumin, if using. Pulse to a thick, coarse-textured paste, then add just enough of the yogurt to create a spreadable pâté. (Alternatively, if you do not own a food processor, mash the ingredients together with the back of a fork to serve as a chunky bean pâté.)

- Scrape the pâté into a bowl, stir in the parsley, then season to taste and serve with plenty of hot toast, garnished with extra parsley.

Bean and Parsley Patties

Mix 2 (15 oz) cans beans, rinsed and drained, with 2 tablespoons tomato paste, 1 tablespoon mayonnaise, 1 teaspoon ground cumin, 2 tablespoons chopped parsley, and a pinch of salt and black pepper in a food processor to a coarse paste. Use your hands to shape it into 16 patties. Heat 2 tablespoons olive or vegetable oil in a skillet and cook the patties for 2–3 minutes on each side. Meanwhile, stir 2 teaspoons lemon juice into ⅔ cup plain or Greek yogurt, ½ teaspoon cumin, and 2 tablespoons chopped parsley. Season, then serve with the patties and pita breads.

Bean and Parsley Stew

Heat 2 tablespoons oil in a large saucepan and cook 1 sliced red onion and 1 chopped green bell pepper over medium heat for 7–8 minutes. Add 2 sliced garlic cloves and cook for 1–2 minutes, until softened. Stir 1 teaspoon each of ground coriander and cumin into the pan and cook for 1 minute, then add 1 g (14½ oz) can diced tomatoes, 1 (15 oz) can drained cannellini, cranberry, or lima beans, 2 tablespoons tomato paste, and 1¼ cups hot vegetable stock. Bring to a boil, then simmer gently for 10–12 minutes, until slightly thickened. Add

2 cups canned fava beans, rinsed and drained, or 1⅓ cups fresh or frozen fava beans and ¼ cup coarsely chopped parsley. Season to taste and simmer for 4–5 minutes, until the beans are tender. Spoon into 4 warm dishes and serve sprinkled with extra chopped parsley and plenty of crusty bread.

STU-BREA-MAO

Smoked Salmon and Chive Mayonnaise

Serves 2 as a light lunch or snack or 4 as a appetizer

4 oz smoked sliced salmon
1 teaspoon lemon juice
3 tablespoons mayonnaise
2 teaspoons chopped chives
 (optional), plus extra to garnish
salt and black pepper

To serve

whole-wheat bread, toasted
lemon wedges (optional)

- Place the smoked salmon in the bowl of a small food processor or mini chopper and add the lemon juice, mayonnaise, chives, if using, and a generous pinch of black pepper. Blend until the salmon is finely chopped but not completely smooth. (Alternatively, if you do not have a food processor, chop the smoked salmon as finely as possible by hand, then place it in a bowl and stir in the other ingredients, mixing well to combine.)

- Scrape the mixture into a small bowl and season with salt to taste. Spread the mixture onto the toast and garnish with chives, if using. Serve with lemon wedges, if desired.

Fresh Salmon and Chive Burgers

Finely chop 8 oz boned and skinned salmon fillet in a food processor (or chop the salmon finely by hand). Finely chop 2 scallions (optional) and add to the salmon with 2 tablespoons mayonnaise or tartar sauce, 1 tablespoon chopped chives, and black pepper. Pulse until well combined, then shape into 2 patties. Heat 2 tablespoons oil in a nonstick skillet and cook over medium heat for 4–5 minutes on each side, until just cooked. Serve on ciabatta rolls with sweet chili sauce and salad greens or with rice and lemon wedges.

Canned Salmon and Chive Fish

Cakes Dice 3 peeled Yukon gold or russet potatoes and cook in a saucepan of lightly salted water for about 10 minutes, until tender but firm. Drain well and set aside, uncovered, to cool slightly. Meanwhile, drain and flake the salmon from 1 (6 oz) can into a bowl with the finely grated rind of ½ lemon (optional), 2 tablespoons tartar sauce or mayonnaise, and 1 tablespoon finely chopped chives. Season generously with plenty of black pepper, then add the potatoes and mash lightly to combine. Form into 4 small fish cakes, coat in 2–3 tablespoons dried bread crumbs, then chill for about 12 minutes until slightly firm. Heat 2 tablespoons vegetable or olive oil in a nonstick skillet and cook the fish cakes over medium heat for about 5 minutes, turning once, until crisp and golden. Serve with salad greens and lemon wedges, if desired.

STU-BREA-WAF

30 Carrot and Feta Potato Cakes

Serves 2

1 large carrot, peeled and diced
3 Yukon gold or russet potatoes,
  peeled and diced
1 medium egg, lightly beaten
½ cup crumbled feta cheese
1 teaspoon ground cumin
1 tablespoon chopped parsley
  (optional)
2 scallions, chopped
flour, for dusting
3–4 tablespoons vegetable oil
salt and black pepper
2 poached or fried eggs, to serve
  (optional)

- Bring a large saucepan of lightly salted water to a boil and cook the carrots and potatoes for about 12 minutes, until tender. Drain well and mash together until crushed but not completely smooth. Set aside to cool, uncovered, for at least 10 minutes.

- While the potatoes and carrots are cooling, add the beaten egg, feta, cumin, parsley, onion, and a pinch each of salt and black pepper to the pan and mix well to combine. Use flour-dusted hands to form the mixture into 4 patties.

- Place the oil in a large nonstick skillet and pan-fry the patties gently for about 3 minutes on each side, until crisp and golden. Drain on paper towels and serve with fried or poached eggs, if desired.

Feta and Parsley Dip with Carrot Sticks In a bowl, mash ⅔ cup crumbled feta cheese with 1 tablespoon chopped parsley, 3 tablespoons crème fraîche, 1 teaspoon lemon juice, and a generous pinch of black pepper. Scrape into an attractive serving dish and serve immediately with sticks of raw carrots and toasted pita bread, if desired.

Baked Mashed Carrots and Potatoes with Feta Place 1 cup cooked leftover potatoes and 1⅓ cups cooked leftover carrots in a bowl. (Alternatively, use a 14½ oz can new potatoes, drained, and a 14½ oz can sliced carrots, drained.) Coarsely mash with the egg, cumin, feta cheese, parsley, and scallions, as above. Press into a greased, shallow ovenproof dish and cook in a preheated oven, at 425°F, for 12–15 minutes, until crisp and golden. Serve hot with a fried or poached egg, if desired.

10 Thai Broiled Chicken Sandwich

Serves 2

8 oz skinless chicken strips

1 tablespoon Thai red or green
    curry paste

2 tablespoons plain yogurt

1 tablespoon mango chutney
    or plain yogurt

1 ciabatta bread, split lengthwise

small handful of shredded
    iceberg lettuce

¼ cucumber, sliced

- Place the chicken strips in a bowl with the curry paste and plain yogurt. Mix together to combine, then arrange on the rack of an aluminum foil-lined broiler pan and slide under a preheated medium-hot broiler. Broil for 7–8 minutes, turning once, until cooked through and lightly charred.

- Meanwhile, spread the mango chutney or plain yogurt inside the ciabatta bread and top with the lettuce and sliced cucumber. Add the cooked chicken fillets, then cut the bread into 4 to serve.

Thai Curry Noodle Soup

Heat 1 tablespoon vegetable oil in a medium saucepan or wok and cook 3 chopped scallions and 2 chopped garlic cloves gently for 2–3 minutes, until softened. Stir in 1 tablespoon green or red Thai curry paste for 2 minutes, then pour in 1 cup coconut milk and 1½ cups hot chicken or vegetable stock. Bring to a boil and simmer gently for 7–8 minutes. Add 2 cups snow peas or 1 cup fine green beans and 8 oz medium noodles and simmer gently according to the package directions until the noodles are just tender. Lift out the noodles and pile them into bowls, then pour the fragrant soup over the noodles. Garnish with cilantro leaves, if desired.

Thai Curry Rice Bowl

Heat 2 tablespoons vegetable oil in a skillet and add 1 coarsely chopped onion. Stir-fry for 4–5 minutes, until beginning to color. Cut 8 oz skinless, boneless chicken thigh into bite-size pieces and add to the skillet for about 10 minutes, stirring frequently, until lightly golden and almost cooked. Stir 1–2 tablespoons (depending on heat required) Thai green curry paste into the skillet and stir-fry for 1 minute, stirring constantly to prevent burning. Pour 1 cup coconut milk and ½ cup hot chicken stock into the skillet and simmer gently for about 10 minutes to let the flavors develop. Serve spooned over bowls of jasmine or long-grain rice, garnished with cilantro leaves, if desired.

30 Sausage and Cheese Rolls

Serves 4

1 sheet ready-to-bake
   puff pastry
3 tablespoons cream cheese
   or cream cheese with chives,
   at room temperature
½ small red onion, finely
   chopped, or 2 finely
   chopped scallions
1 cup shredded American
   or cheddar cheese
8 herb-flavor link sausages
1 medium egg, beaten

- Place the pastry sheet on a clean surface and spread the cream cheese thinly over the surface. Sprinkle with the chopped onion and ¾ cup of the shredded cheese.

- Cut the pastry lengthwise into 2 long strips and arrange 4 sausages, end to end, along the center of each strip. Roll up the pastry strips to create 2 long log-shape rolls, then cut each roll into 4 individual sausage rolls.

- Arrange the sausage rolls on baking sheets lined with aluminum foil, make 2–3 small cuts in the top of each one, then brush with beaten egg and sprinkle with the remaining shredded cheese.

- Bake in a preheated oven, at 425°F, for 18–22 minutes or until the sausages are cooked through and the pastry is puffed up and golden. Serve warm or cold as part of a light lunch or brunch.

1 Sausage and Cheese Baguette

Place 4 cut pieces of French bread, cut side up, on a baking sheet and slide under a broiler preheated to a medium setting. Broil for 2–3 minutes, until lightly toasted. Meanwhile, beat 1 egg in a large bowl and mix well with 1¼ cups shredded American or cheddar cheese, 2 teaspoons Worcestershire sauce, 1 teaspoon whole-grain mustard, and 2 tablespoons milk or beer. Thickly slice 8 frankfurters or leftover cooked link sausages and arrange over the toasted baguette. Spoon the cheesy topping over the sausages and return to the broiler for 2–3 minutes, until the cheese is melted and golden. Serve hot.

2 Sausage and Cheese Turnovers

Cut a sheet of ready-to-bake puff pastry into quarters and arrange on a baking sheet. Brush each quarter with 1 teaspoon mild mustard and sprinkle with ½ cup grated American or cheddar cheese. Top each one with 2 frankfurters, then fold over the pastry and brush with beaten egg. Bake in a preheated oven, at 425°F, for about 15 minutes or until the pastry is puffed up and golden. Serve hot or cold.

QuickCook

Brain Food Meals

Recipes listed by cooking time

30

20

10

Herbed Pan-Fried Salmon

Serves 4

6 tablespoons butter

2 scallions, finely sliced

3 tablespoons mixed chopped herbs (such as parsley, chives, chervil, and tarragon)

1 tablespoon drained capers, rinsed (optional)

1 teaspoon finely grated lemon rind

1 tablespoon lemon juice

4 (5 oz) boneless salmon fillets, with skin

2 teaspoons olive or vegetable oil

To serve

steamed couscous

lemon wedges

- Melt the butter in a saucepan and cook the scallions over medium-low heat for 2–3 minutes, until softened. Stir in the chopped herbs, capers, if using, and the lemon rind and juice, then remove from the heat and set aside.

- Meanwhile, rub a little oil over the salmon fillets and heat a skillet until hot. Cook the salmon, skin side down, over medium-high heat for 3–4 minutes or until the skin is crispy. Carefully turn over the fillets and cook for another 3–4 minutes, until just cooked but still slightly pink in the middle. Cover with aluminum foil and set aside to rest somewhere warm for 2–3 minutes.

- Arrange the salmon fillets in warm dishes and drizzle with the herb butter. Serve immediately with steamed couscous and lemon wedges.

 Herbed Smoked Salmon Pasta

Cook 1 lb quick-cooking pasta (such as thin spaghetti) in a large saucepan of lightly salted boiling water according to the package directions until just tender. Drain the pasta and return to the pan, then toss with ¼ cup pesto, 4 oz sliced smoked salmon, 1 tablespoon lemon juice, and 3 tablespoons crème fraîche. Season with black pepper and pile into warm bowls to serve.

 Herbed Baked Salmon

Place 6 tablespoons softened butter in a bowl and mix with 3 tablespoons mixed chopped herbs, 1 teaspoon finely grated lemon rind, and a pinch each of salt and black pepper. Smear the herb butter over 4 chunky, boneless salmon fillets and arrange in an aluminum foil-lined ovenproof dish. Cover with foil, scrunching together the edges to seal, then bake in a preheated oven, at 350°F, for 18–20 minutes, until the salmon is just cooked but still slightly pink in the middle. Remove from the oven and set aside to rest for 2–3 minutes, then sprinkle with 1 tablespoon drained capers and 2 sliced scallions and serve with steamed couscous or new potatoes, with lemon wedges and arugula leaves, if desired.

Sizzling Beef and Broccoli Stir-Fry

Serves 2

1 tablespoon vegetable or
  sesame oil
5 oz top sirloin steak, fat
  removed and cut into thin strips
1 onion, sliced
1 red bell pepper, cut into strips
1⅔ cups small broccoli florets
small handful of bean sprouts
  (optional)
6 oz dried fine egg noodles
½ cup black bean stir-fry sauce,
  or similar

- Heat the oil in a skillet or wok and cook the steak over medium-high heat for about 2 minutes, stirring occasionally, until browned, then remove with a slotted spoon and set aside.

- Return the skillet to the heat, adding a little extra oil if necessary, and stir-fry the onion and bell pepper for 2–3 minutes, until they begin to soften. Stir the broccoli into the skillet and cook for another 2 minutes, then add the bean sprouts, if using, and cook for 1–2 minutes, just until they begin to wilt.

- Meanwhile, cook the noodles according to the package directions until just tender.

- Return the beef to the skillet to reheat, add the black bean sauce, then transfer the drained noodles to the skillet and toss quickly to combine. Pile into 2 warm bowls to serve.

Quick Beef Chow Mein with Broccoli

Heat 2 tablespoons vegetable oil in a skillet and cook the beef as above, then remove with a slotted spoon and set aside. Add 2 cups broccoli florets to the skillet with 2 sliced scallions and stir-fry for 2–3 minutes, until almost tender. Transfer 8 oz noodles, freshly cooked, into the skillet and stir-fry for another 2–3 minutes, until tender and hot. Return the beef to the skillet with ½ cup chow mein stir-fry sauce and stir to heat. Heap into bowls and serve immediately.

Marinated Beef with Broccoli and Brown Rice

Place 1 thick (8 oz) top sirloin steak into a dish and pour 2 tablespoons sweet teriyaki marinade mixed with 2 teaspoons peeled and grated fresh ginger root and 1 crushed garlic clove over the top. Rub the marinade all over the steak and set aside in the refrigerator for at least 10 minutes. Heat 1 tablespoon vegetable oil a skillet and cook the steak over medium-high heat for 3–4 minutes on each side, until browned but still pink. Remove from the skillet and set aside somewhere warm to rest. Clean the skillet and return to medium heat with 1 tablespoon oil. Stir-fry 1⅔ cups broccoli florets for 3–4 minutes, until just tender, then remove the broccoli from the skillet. Slice the beef thickly, then toss with the broccoli and arrange over 2 bowls of cooked brown rice. Pour ¼ cup sweet teriyaki marinade into the skillet to heat, then remove from the heat and drizzle the heated marinade over the beef and broccoli to serve.

Citrus Chicken Salad

Serves 2

1 orange
4 cooked roasted chicken thighs
1 bunch watercress
   or 3 cups arugula
1 avocado, pitted, peeled,
   and sliced
2 teaspoons walnut or olive oil
shelled walnut pieces (optional)

- Place the orange on a cutting board and use a small sharp knife to cut off the top and bottom so that you cut right through the peel and outside pith to the flesh. Now cut the remaining peel and pith away from the flesh, cutting in strips downward, following the curve of the orange. Cut the orange into fleshy segments, using a sharp knife to carefully cut either side of the inside pith. Discard the peel and pith, keeping only the segments.

- Slice or shred the cooked chicken thighs, discarding the bones and skin, if preferred. Divide the watercress between 2 plates and arrange the orange segments, chicken, and sliced avocado attractively over the watercress. Drizzle with walnut oil and sprinkle with a few walnut pieces, if desired.

---

2 Citrus Chicken Couscous

Place 2 chicken breasts between 2 pieces of plastic wrap and batter with a rolling pin or the bottom of a saucepan to flatten. Place in a dish with 2 teaspoons finely grated lemon rind, 2 tablespoons olive oil, 1 teaspoon chopped thyme leaves (optional), 1 crushed garlic clove, and a generous pinch of black pepper. Rub the chicken well with all the flavors. Heat a large dry skillet and cook the chicken over medium heat for 3–4 minutes each side or until golden and the juices run clear when the flesh is pierced with the tip of a sharp knife. Remove from the heat, cover, and rest

for 2–3 minutes. Meanwhile, place ¾ cup couscous in a bowl with a small pat of butter and 1 tablespoon lemon juice, then pour ½ cup boiling chicken stock over the grains. Cover and set aside for 5–8 minutes or until the grains are tender and the liquid has been absorbed. Fluff up the couscous with a fork, then spoon into 2 warm dishes and top with the chicken and its juices to serve.

3 Citrus Baked Chicken

Wrap 4 bacon slices around 2 chicken breasts and pan-fry in 1 tablespoon olive oil over medium-high heat for 2 minutes on each side, until browned. Meanwhile, warm 1 cup orange juice in a saucepan with ½ teaspoon dried thyme and 2 teaspoons whole-grain mustard. Put the chicken in an ovenproof dish, pour the juice over the chicken, and bake in a preheated oven, at 400°F, for about 20 minutes, until the chicken is cooked through. Slice thickly, arrange on 2 warm plates, drizzle with the orangey juices, and serve with an arugula and avocado salad.

Vegetable Pasta Bowl

Serves 4

¼ cup olive or vegetable oil
2 garlic cloves, sliced
1 lb pasta shells or bows
4 cups broccoli florets
2 cups halved green beans
12 cherry tomatoes, halved
2–3 tablespoons lemon juice
salt and black pepper

- Warm the oil in a small saucepan and add the sliced garlic. Heat the pan gently for 1–2 minutes to soften the garlic and flavor the oil. Remove from the heat and set aside to steep.

- Bring a saucepan of lightly salted water to a boil and cook the pasta according to the package directions. Add the broccoli and green beans for the final 3–4 minutes of cooking time. When the vegetables and pasta are just tender, drain well, reserving 2 tablespoons of the cooking liquid.

- Stir the cherry tomatoes gently into the pasta and vegetables with the warm garlicky oil, reserved water, and the lemon juice, to taste. Season with a pinch of salt and plenty of black pepper, then spoon into 4 bowls to serve.

Vegetable Pasta Soup

Heat 2 tablespoons oil in a saucepan and cook 2 sliced garlic cloves gently for 1 minute. Pour in 3¾ cups hot vegetable stock, bring to a boil, add 6 oz vermicelli or other small pasta shape, and simmer for 2–3 minutes. Add 3 cups broccoli florets and 2 shredded zucchini. Return to a boil and simmer for 3–5 minutes, until the vegetables and pasta are tender. Serve immediately with plenty of crusty bread.

Vegetable Pasta Casserole

Cook 12 oz penne in a large saucepan of lightly salted boiling water according to the package directions until just tender. Drain and return the pasta to the pan. Meanwhile, heat 2 tablespoons olive or vegetable oil in a large skillet and cook 1 chopped onion and 1 chopped red bell pepper for 6–7 minutes over medium-high heat until softened. Add 1 shredded zucchini, 2 cups sliced mushrooms, and 1⅔ cups small broccoli florets (optional) and cook for another 2–3 minutes, until the vegetables begin to soften. Stir in 1⅔ cups tomato sauce or chopped tomatoes and simmer gently for 2–3 minutes, until the vegetables are almost tender. Pour the sauce over the drained pasta with ⅔ cup crème fraîche or heavy cream (optional, for a creamier bake), then season and transfer into a large ovenproof dish. Top with 1 cup shredded cheese and bake in a preheated oven, at 425°F, for 12–15 minutes, until bubbling and golden.

Indian-Inspired Beef and Sweet Potato with Spinach

Serves 4

3 tablespoons vegetable oil

1 lb stir-fry beef strips

1 red bell pepper, cut into large chunks

1 onion, thickly sliced

1 large sweet potato, peeled and diced

2 cups Indian curry cooking sauce

3 tomatoes, cut into wedges

1 (6 oz) package spinach, washed and coarsely chopped

- Heat 2 tablespoons of the oil in a saucepan set over medium-high heat and cook the beef for 3–4 minutes, stirring occasionally, until browned and just cooked through. Remove from the pan with a slotted spoon and set aside. Return the pan to the heat.

- Add the remaining oil to the pan and cook the bell pepper, onion, and sweet potato for 5–6 minutes, stirring frequently, until lightly browned and softened.

- Stir the curry sauce into the pan with the tomato wedges, then reduce the heat, cover, and simmer gently for about 15 minutes or until the vegetables are tender and the sauce has thickened slightly.

- Return the beef to the pan, add the spinach, and stir over the heat for 1–2 minutes, until the beef is hot and the spinach has wilted. Serve immediately.

 Curried Beef Stir-Fry with Spinach Heat 2 tablespoons oil in a skillet and cook 1 lb beef stir-fry strips over high heat for 2 minutes, until browned all over. Add 1 thinly sliced onion and cook for 2 minutes. Reduce the heat, stir in 2 tablespoons curry paste, 1¾ cups coconut milk and 1 cup hot beef or vegetable stock. Simmer gently for 2 minutes. Stir in 1 (6 oz) package coarsely chopped spinach until just wilted. Serve with rice or warm crusty bread.

 Indian Hamburgers with Spinach In a bowl, combine 1 lb ground beef with 1 small finely chopped onion, 1 tablespoon curry paste, and 2 tablespoons chopped cilantro or parsley. Mix really well with your hands, then shape into 4 patties. Heat 2 tablespoons vegetable oil in a skillet and cook the patties over medium heat for 4–5 minutes on each side, until cooked through but still juicy. Meanwhile, if desired, mix 1 teaspoon lemon juice, ½ teaspoon ground cumin, and a pinch each of salt and black pepper into ¼ cup plain yogurt. Arrange the cooked burgers in burger buns, pita breads, or wraps and top each one with a small handful of young spinach leaves. Serve with sliced cucumber and a dollop of the spiced yogurt or some mango chutney.

Flaked Mackerel and Green Pepper Couscous

Serves 4

1½ cups couscous

1¼ cups hot vegetable stock
   or water

1 green bell pepper, diced

2 scallions, finely sliced

small bunch of parsley, chopped

2 smoked mackerel fillets, skinned
   and flaked

For the dressing

1 tablespoon harissa
   or tomato paste

¼ cup olive or vegetable oil

1½ tablespoons lemon juice

- Place the couscous in a bowl and pour the boiling stock over the grains. Cover and set aside for 5–6 minutes, until just tender.

- Combine the dressing ingredients in a small bowl.

- Fork the bell pepper, onions, and parsley through the couscous with 2 tablespoons of the dressing. Spoon the couscous salad onto plates and sprinkle with the flaked mackerel. Serve with the dressing on the side, for drizzling on top.

 Broiled Mackerel with Red Peppers and Couscous Mix ¼ cup vegetable oil with 2 teaspoons grated lemon rind, 3 crushed garlic cloves, and 1 tablespoon grated fresh ginger root. Put 8 boned mackerel fillets and 2 red bell peppers, cut into wedges, in a shallow dish. Pour the marinade over them, mixing to coat. Set aside for 5–10 minutes. Arrange the mackerel fillets and bell peppers on the rack of an aluminum foil-lined broiler pan, skin side up, then cook under a broiler preheated to its highest setting for 4–5 minutes, turning once. Serve with steamed couscous, drizzled with any juices.

 Green Pepper, Mackerel, and Lentil Curry with Spinach Cut 1 lb boned mackerel fillets into large chunks and place in a bowl with 3 tablespoons curry paste (such as tikka masala paste). Mix thoroughly to coat the mackerel in the spices, then set aside. Now heat 2 tablespoons vegetable oil in a large skillet and cook 1 chopped green bell pepper over medium heat for 6–7 minutes. Add 2 chopped garlic cloves and 1 tablespoon peeled and chopped fresh ginger root (optional) and cook for another 2 minutes, until softened. Scrape the mackerel into the skillet and stir over the heat for 2 minutes to cook the spices. Pour 1 cup coconut milk, 1¼ cups hot vegetable stock, and the rinsed and drained lentils from 1 (15 oz) can into the skillet, bring to a boil, then reduce the heat and simmer gently for about 12 minutes, until the fish is cooked and the curry has thickened. Stir in 1 (10 oz) package thawed, frozen spinach and cook for another 1–2 minutes, until hot, then serve spooned over cooked couscous or rice or with plenty of warm crusty bread.

10 Broiled Harissa Lamb with Pita

Serves 2

2 (5 oz) lamb cutlets

1 teaspoon finely grated
lemon rind

1 tablespoon olive oil

2–4 teaspoons harissa

¼ cup hummus

2 whole-wheat pita breads

To serve (optional)

lemon wedges

arugula leaves

- Place the lamb cutlets in a dish with the lemon rind, oil, and 1–2 teaspoons harissa and rub to coat. Arrange the coated lamb on the rack of an aluminum foil-lined broiler pan and cook under a broiler preheated to a medium-high setting for 5–7 minutes, turning once, until cooked but still slightly pink in the middle. Remove and set aside to rest for 1–2 minutes.

- Meanwhile, stir 1–2 teaspoons harissa into the hummus. Lightly toast the pita breads in a toaster, then arrange on warm plates and top with a dollop of hummus. Arrange the lamb cutlets on top of the hummus, drizzled with any juices. Serve with lemon wedges and arugula leaves, if desired.

2 Broiled Harissa Lamb Skewers

Mix 1 tablespoon harissa with 2 tablespoons plain yogurt, 1 teaspoon finely grated lemon rind, 1 tablespoon chopped mint (optional), and ½ teaspoon cumin seeds. Mix well with 4 oz cubed lamb to coat, then set aside for 5 minutes. Thread onto skewers, arrange on the rack of an aluminum foil-lined broiler pan, and cook under a broiler preheated to a medium-high setting for 6–8 minutes, until charred but still slightly pink. Rest for 1–2 minutes, then serve with couscous and hummus.

3 Harissa Lamb Koftas with Sesame Seeds

Place 8 oz ground lamb in a bowl with ½ teaspoon ground cumin, 1 teaspoon finely grated lemon rind, and 2 teaspoons harissa and mix thoroughly with your hands to form 8–10 slightly flattened meatball shapes. Chill in the refrigerator for 10 minutes. Meanwhile, boil 1 cup rinsed long-grain rice in a saucepan of lightly salted water for according to the package directions until just tender. Heat 2 tablespoons oil in a skillet and cook the flattened lamb balls

gently for 8–10 minutes, until cooked and golden. Remove the skillet from the heat and sprinkle with 2 teaspoons sesame seeds, shaking the skillet to coat. Drain the rice and spoon onto 2 warm plates. Top with the lamb koftas, then sprinkle with 1 tablespoon chopped parsley (optional) and 1 teaspoon sesame seeds. Serve immediately with a generous dollop of harissa hummus, made as above.

Red Pepper, Kidney Bean, and Spinach Stew

Serves 4

3 tablespoons olive or vegetable oil

2 large red bell peppers, cut into large pieces

3 garlic cloves, sliced

2 teaspoons ground cumin or Mexican spice mix, such as fajita seasoning (optional)

2 tablespoons tomato paste

1¾ cups hot vegetable stock

1 (14½ oz) can diced tomatoes

2½ cups rinsed and drained, canned kidney beans

1 (10 oz) package frozen spinach, defrosted and drained

salt and black pepper

- Heat the oil in a saucepan and cook the bell peppers and garlic over medium heat for 5–6 minutes, stirring frequently, until softened.

- Stir in the cumin, if using, and cook for 1 minute before adding the tomato paste, hot stock, diced tomatoes, and kidney beans. Bring to a boil, season to taste, then cover and simmer gently for 10–12 minutes, until thickened slightly. Stir in the spinach for the final minute of cooking, then ladle into bowls to serve.

 Mixed Bell Pepper, Kidney Bean, and Spinach Salad In a bowl, mix 1 red and 1 green pepper, finely chopped, ½ cucumber, diced, and 1 small bunch of chopped cilantro or parsley with 1 (15 oz) can kidney beans, rinsed and drained. Drizzle with 3 tablespoons each of oil and lime juice, then season to taste and toss gently with 1 (6 oz) package young spinach to serve.

 Red Pepper and Kidney Bean Soup Cook the bell peppers and garlic as above until softened. Add the ground cumin and cook for a minute, then pour in 3 cups hot vegetable stock, 2 cups tomato puree or sauce and 2 (15 oz) cans kidney beans, rinsed and drained, reserving about 1 cup of the beans. Season with a pinch each of salt and black pepper, then cover, bring to a boil, and simmer for about 15 minutes, until slightly thickened. Use a handheld immersion blender to blend the soup (alternatively, if you don't have a blender, serve it as a chunky bean soup), then stir through the reserved beans and ½ (10 oz) package defrosted chopped spinach and heat through. Ladle into bowls to serve, sprinkled with chopped parsley, if desired.

Sweet Chili Salmon Fish Cakes

Serves 2

8 oz chunky boneless and skinless
  salmon fillet, coarsely diced
1 tablespoon sweet chili sauce
1 small garlic clove, crushed
  (optional)
2 scallions, finely chopped
2 tablespoons finely chopped
  cilantro
1 teaspoon finely grated lime
  rind (optional)
2 tablespoons vegetable oil

- Place the diced salmon in a food processor with the chili sauce, garlic, scallions, cilanto, and lime rind and pulse quickly until chopped together, but not smooth. (Alternatively, if you do not own a food processor, chop the salmon as finely as possible before mixing with the remaining ingredients.) Scrape into a bowl, then use damp hands to shape into 2 patties. Arrange on a plate, cover with plastic wrap, and chill in the refrigerator for 10–12 minutes, until slightly firm.

- Heat the oil in a large nonstick skillet and cook the fish cakes over medium heat for 5–6 minutes each side, until golden and cooked through. Serve immediately with steamed or egg fried rice.

 Smoked Salmon and Sweet Chili Baguettes In a small bowl, mix 1 tablespoon sweet chili sauce with 2 tablespoons cream cheese and 1 tablespoon chopped cilantro (optional). Spread over 2 split individual sandwich baguettes and sprinkle with 1 small, ripe but firm avocado, diced, and 1 finely sliced scallion. Top each baguette with about 2 oz sliced smoked salmon, then squeeze with a little lime juice (optional). Season with black pepper, garnish with a few arugula leaves, then serve with additional sweet chili sauce, if desired.

 Sweet Chili Salmon Quesadillas Rub a little oil over 1 chunky (7 oz) salmon fillet and season with a little salt and black pepper. Heat a nonstick skillet and cook the salmon fillet for about 4 minutes on each side, until just cooked through. Cover with aluminum foil and set aside to rest for 2–3 minutes. Arrange 2 large, soft tortilla wraps on a clean surface and sprinkle with 2 thinly sliced scallions and 1 ripe but firm avocado, diced. Flake the salmon over the avocado and drizzle each tortilla with 2 teaspoons sweet chili sauce, then top each one with a second tortilla. Toast the quesadillas, one at a time, in a large, dry skillet for about 4 minutes, carefully turning over halfway through cooking, until toasted and browned. Cut into slices and serve hot with lime wedges, if desired.

Spiced Vegetable and Chickpea Soup

Serves 4

2 tablespoons olive or
   vegetable oil
1 onion, chopped
1 green or red bell pepper,
   chopped
1 eggplant, diced
2 teaspoons peeled and chopped
   fresh ginger root
1 teaspoon dried red pepper flakes
6 tomatoes, coarsely diced
3¾ cups hot vegetable stock
1 (15 oz) can chickpeas,
   rinsed and drained
salt and black pepper

- Heat the oil in a large saucepan and cook the vegetables and ginger for 7–8 minutes, until slightly softened. Add the dried red pepper flakes, tomatoes, hot stock, and chickpeas and bring to a boil. Reduce the heat and simmer gently for about 10 minutes, until the vegetables are tender.

- Use a handheld immersion blender to blend until smooth. (Alternatively, if you don't have a blender, serve it as a chunky soup.) Season to taste, then ladle into mugs or bowls to serve.

Spiced Chickpea Hummus with

Crudités Heat 2 tablespoons olive or vegetable oil in a small skillet and cook 2 chopped garlic cloves and 1 teaspoon dried red pepper flakes over low heat for 2–3 minutes, until softened. Scrape into a food processor with 1 teaspoon ground cumin, 1 tablespoon lemon juice, and 2 tablespoons plain yogurt. Process until smooth, then season to taste, scrape into a bowl, and serve with plenty of raw vegetable dippers (such as carrot, cucumber, and celery sticks, broccoli and cauliflower florets, cherry tomatoes, button mushrooms, radishes, and mixed bell pepper strips).

Spiced Eggplant with Chickpeas

Cut 2 eggplants into bite-size pieces, then mix in a bowl with 1 chopped onion, 1 chopped green bell pepper, and 1 tablespoon harissa. Heat 3 tablespoons olive or vegetable oil in a large saucepan and cook the vegetables over medium heat for about 6–7 minutes, stirring frequently, until slightly softened. Stir in 2 (14½ oz) cans diced tomatoes and 1 (15 oz) can chickpeas, rinsed and drained. Season to taste, then cover and simmer gently for about 15 minutes until the vegetables are tender. Serve the spiced eggplant with couscous, if desired.

1 Healthy Green Bean and Broccoli Salad

Serves 2

2–3 cups mixture of broccoli
florets and fine green beans

1 (15 oz) canned cranberry beans
or chickpeas, rinsed and drained

1 celery stick, finely chopped

½ small red onion, finely sliced

1 small ripe avocado, pitted,
peeled, and diced

1 tablespoon sunflower seeds

For the dressing

1 tablespoon lime or lemon juice

2 tablespoons peanut or
vegetable oil

1 tablespoon light soy sauce

- Cook the green beans and broccoli in a saucepan of lightly salted boiling water for 2–3 minutes, until lightly cooked. Drain and cool under cold water.

- Meanwhile, combine the canned beans in a bowl with the celery, onion, and avocado.

- Whisk together the dressing ingredients in a small bowl.

- Add the cold beans to the salad and gently fold through the dressing. Spoon into a serving dish and sprinkle with the sunflower seeds.

2 Healthy Green Bean and Broccoli Bowl

Heat 2 tablespoons peanut or vegetable oil in a skillet or wok and cook 1 sliced onion and 1 sliced red pepper over high heat for 3–4 minutes, until they begin to soften. Add 1 chopped garlic clove and 1 teaspoon peeled and chopped fresh ginger root for another minute. Stir 1½ cups halved green beans into the skillet with 1⅔ cups small broccoli florets and stir-fry for 3–4 minutes, until the vegetables are almost tender. Now stir 1½ cups bean sprouts into the skillet and cook for another 2–3 minutes, until the vegetables are just tender. Remove from the heat, toss with 1 tablespoon light soy sauce, and pile into bowls to serve, sprinkled with a teaspoon of sesame seeds and extra soy sauce, if desired.

3 Healthy Rice, Green Bean, and Broccoli Bowl

Cook 1 cup brown rice in a saucepan of boiling water for 20–25 minutes, until tender. Cool under cold water and drain. Meanwhile, cook 1 cup fine green beans and 1⅔ cups broccoli florets in a saucepan of boiling water for 2–3 minutes, until almost tender. Cool under cold water and drain. Combine ½ (15 oz) can kidney beans, drained and rinsed, with 1 cup canned corn kernels, drained, and 1 sliced scallion. Add the rice with the broccoli, 2 tablespoons chopped cilantro, and 1 tablespoon lime or lemon juice. Stir to combine, then spoon into dishes to serve.

Sage and Lemon Stir-Fried Turkey

Serves 2

2 tablespoons olive or
    vegetable oil
8 oz stir-fry turkey strips
finely grated rind and juice of
    ½ lemon
1 garlic clove, crushed
2 teaspoons shredded sage
    leaves, plus extra to garnish
1⅓ cups hot vegetable stock
1 cup bulgur wheat
steamed green beans or snow
    peas, to serve (optional)

- In a bowl, combine 1 tablespoon of the oil with the turkey strips, lemon rind and juice, garlic, and sage and set aside in the refrigerator to marinate for 5 minutes.

- Meanwhile, bring the vegetable stock to a boil in a saucepan and add the bulgur wheat. Cover and simmer for 7 minutes, then turn off the heat and set aside for about 10 minutes, until the grains are tender and the liquid has been absorbed.

- Heat a skillet with the remaining oil and scrape the marinated turkey into the skillet. Stir-fry gently for about 10 minutes or until the turkey is cooked through. Fork gently into the cooked bulgur and spoon into dishes. Serve garnished with sage leaves, with steamed green beans or snow peas, if desired.

Sage, Lemon, and Turkey Ciabatta

Place ½ cup cream cheese in a bowl with 2 teaspoons finely chopped sage, 1 teaspoon each of finely grated lemon rind and juice, ½ small crushed garlic clove (optional), and a pinch each of salt and black pepper. Mash with a fork until combined, then spread thickly over the cut bottoms of 2 ciabatta rolls. Top with about 4 oz cooked, sliced turkey and fill each roll with a small handful of arugula or young spinach. Serve cold or toast in a panini machine for 2–3 minutes, until lightly toasted.

Sage and Lemon Baked Turkey

Cutlets Mix 1 tablespoon olive or vegetable oil with the finely grated rind and juice of ½ lemon, 1 crushed garlic clove, and 2 teaspoons shredded sage leaves in an ovenproof dish, then add 2 thick (5 oz) turkey cutlets and rub the marinade all over. Set aside in the refrigerator for 5 minutes. Heat another 1 tablespoon of olive or vegetable oil in a skillet and cook the turkey cutlets for about 2 minutes on each side until golden, then return to the ovenproof dish. Add ¼ cup dry white wine, then cover with aluminum foil and bake in a preheated oven, at 375°F, for 15–20 minutes, until the turkey is cooked but not dry, and the juices run clear when the meat is pierced with the tip of a sharp knife. Meanwhile, cook 1 cup bulgur wheat in 1⅓ cups vegetable stock as above. Spoon the bulgur onto warm plates, top with the turkey, and drizzle with the juices. Serve garnished with extra sage leaves and lemon wedges, if desired.

Pasta Casserole with Blue Cheese and Walnuts

Serves 4

12 oz whole-wheat penne or other pasta shape

½ head of broccoli, broken into florets

2 tablespoons olive or vegetable oil

1 cup chopped, shelled walnuts

3 scallions, coarsely sliced (optional)

2 teaspoons chopped sage or 1 teaspoon dried sage

⅔ cup light cream

2 cups diced soft blue cheese (such as dolcelatte, Gorgonzola, or Saint Agur)

- Cook the pasta in a large saucepan of lightly salted boiling water according to the package directions. Add the broccoli for the final 3–4 minutes of cooking time. When the broccoli and pasta are just tender, drain well and return to the pan.

- Meanwhile, heat the oil in a skillet and gently sauté the walnuts and scallions, if using, over medium-low heat for 2–3 minutes, stirring frequently, until golden. Stir in the sage, cream, and 1½ cups of the blue cheese until the cheese has melted and the sauce is creamy. Scrape into the drained pasta and broccoli, mix together, then transfer into an ovenproof dish.

- Sprinkle with the remaining cheese and bake in a preheated oven, at 400°F, for about 15 minutes, until the topping is golden.

 Blue Cheese and Walnut Pasta Salad

Cook 1 lb quick-cooking pasta in a saucepan of lightly salted boiling water according to the package directions, until just tender. Cool under running cold water, drain, and return to the pan. Stir in 3 tablespoons pesto with 2 teaspoons lemon juice and 2 tablespoons crème fraîche or sour cream. Spoon into bowls, then sprinkle with 1⅓ cups crumbled firm blue cheese (such as Stilton) and ½ cup shelled walnut pieces to serve.

 Blue Cheese and Walnut Pasta

Twists Cook 1 lb whole-wheat fusilli in a large saucepan of lightly salted boiling water according to the package directions until just tender. Meanwhile, heat 2 tablespoons olive or vegetable oil in a skillet and cook 3 cups sliced mushrooms over medium heat for 5–6 minutes, stirring occasionally, until golden and tender. Add 2 chopped garlic cloves with 1 cup shelled and chopped walnuts and 3 sliced scallions and cook, stirring frequently, for 2–3 minutes. Pour in ⅔ cup light cream, add 1⅔ cup soft blue cheese, and stir to melt. Remove from the heat and stir in 2 teaspoons lemon juice and a generous pinch each of salt and black pepper. Drain the pasta, return to the pan, and stir in the creamy mushroom and walnut sauce. Spoon the pasta into 4 warm dishes and serve immediately.

Sardine and Three Bean Salad

Serves 4

1 (15 oz) can lima beans
  or cannellini beans, rinsed
  and drained
¾ cup rinsed and drained, canned
  kidney beans or black beans
1½ cups rinsed and drained
  chickpeas or fava beans
2 (3¾ oz) cans sardines,
  drained and flaked
1 red onion, finely chopped
2 celery sticks, finely sliced
  (optional)
1 tablespoons red wine vinegar
3 tablespoons olive oil
salt and black pepper

- Gently mix all of the ingredients together in a large bowl and season to taste.

- Spoon into bowls to serve.

Sardine and Bean Linguine

Heat 2 tablespoons olive oil in a skillet and cook 1 finely chopped red onion, 2 finely chopped celery sticks, and 2 finely chopped garlic cloves gently for 10–12 minutes, until softened but not browned. Stir in 2 (3¾ oz) cans drained sardines and 1 (15 oz) can cranberry beans, rinsed and drained, into the skillet and cook for 2–3 minutes, until hot. Meanwhile, cook 1 lb linguine or spaghetti in a large saucepan of lightly salted boiling water according to the package directions until just tender. Drain the pasta, return it to the pan, then scrape the sardine mixture into the linguine and toss to combine. Pile into warm dishes to serve.

Sardine and Brown Rice Bowl

Cook 1½ cups quick-cooking brown rice in a saucepan of boiling water according to the package directions, until tender. Drain and rinse under cold water to cool. Meanwhile, in a large bowl, combine 1 (15 oz) can kidney beans, rinsed and drained, 1 chopped red bell pepper, 1 small chopped red onion, 2 tablespoons lime juice, 1 tablespoon light soy sauce, 2 tablespoons vegetable oil, and 1 bunch chopped cilantro. Fold through the cold rice and spoon into bowls. Sprinkle with 2 (3¾ oz) cans drained and flaked sardines to serve.

Spicy Chorizo and Tomato Pasta

Serves 4

2 tablespoons olive or
  vegetable oil
8 oz chorizo sausage, diced
2 garlic cloves, chopped
2 (14½ oz) cans diced tomatoes
½ teaspoon dried
  red pepper flakes
1 cup coarsely chopped, drained
  roasted peppers
1 lb pasta shapes
  (such as penne or fusilli)

- Heat the oil in a large skillet or saucepan and cook the chorizo for 3–4 minutes, until lightly golden. Add the remaining ingredients, except the pasta, and bring to a boil. Reduce the heat and simmer gently for 15 minutes, stirring occasionally, until rich and thickened.

- Meanwhile, cook the pasta in a large saucepan of lightly salted boiling water according to the package directions, until just tender. Drain and pile into dishes. Top with the spicy chorizo sauce to serve.

Quick Fried Rice with Tomato and Chorizo
Heat 2 tablespoons olive or vegetable oil in a skillet and add 1 halved and thinly sliced red onion, 2 sliced garlic cloves, 1 seeded and finely chopped red chile (optional), and 8 oz diced chorizo sausage. Cook over medium-high heat for 3–4 minutes, until slightly softened. Stir in 4 cups cooked rice and 1⅓ cups peas (thawed if frozen). Stir over the heat for 2–3 minutes, until piping hot, then stir in 2 seeded and diced tomatoes and spoon into warm dishes to serve.

One-Dish Tomato and Chorizo Jambalaya
Heat 2 tablespoons olive or vegetable oil in a large saucepan and cook 8 oz diced chorizo sausage, 1 chopped red onion, and 1 chopped red bell pepper over medium-high heat for 4–5 minutes, stirring frequently, until slightly browned. Stir in 1 tablespoon Cajun-style spice mix and 1⅓ cups rinsed long-grain rice, then add 1 (14½ oz) can diced tomatoes and 2½ cups boiling stock. Bring to a boil, then reduce the heat, cover with a tight-fitting lid, and simmer gently for about 20 minutes, until the rice is tender and the liquid has been absorbed. Spoon into warm dishes and serve with a few drops of Tabasco sauce and sprinkled with chopped parsley, if desired.

Carrot and Broccoli Vegetable Stir-Fry

Serves 2

1 tablespoon vegetable oil

2½ cups small broccoli florets

2 carrots, peeled and cut into thin batons

2 scallions, cut into ¾ inch lengths

2 cups halved or thickly sliced mushrooms

8 oz medium egg noodles

2 tablespoons sweet chili sauce

1 tablespoon soy sauce, plus extra to serve

- Heat the oil in a large skillet or wok and stir-fry the broccoli and carrot for 3 minutes over medium-hot heat, until the vegetables begin to soften slightly.

- Add the scallions and cook for another 2 minutes, until they are slightly browned, then stir in the mushrooms. Stir-fry for 3–4 minutes, until the mushrooms are just tender.

- Meanwhile, cook the noodles in a saucepan of boiling water according to the package directions, until just tender, and then drain.

- Remove the stir-fried vegetables from the heat, pour in the sweet chili sauce and soy sauce, then add the noodles and toss to coat. Pile into 2 warm bowls and serve immediately with extra soy sauce, if desired.

 Quick Broccoli and Carrot Couscous Place ¾ cup couscous in a bowl with 2 tablespoons butter or 1 tablespoon olive or vegetable oil. Pour ¾ cup boiling vegetable stock over the grains and set aside for 5–7 minutes, until the liquid has been absorbed and the grains are tender. Meanwhile, heat 2 tablespoons vegetable oil in a large skillet or wok and add 1 (12 oz) package broccoli and carrot stir-fry medley to the skillet. Stir-fry for 3–4 minutes, until just tender but still slightly crunchy. Fold into the steamed couscous with 3 tablespoons sweet chili sauce and serve.

 Crunchy Baked Carrots and Broccoli Bring a large saucepan of lightly salted water to a boil. Cut 2 peeled carrots into batons and add these to the water with 2 cups each of broccoli and cauliflower florets. Cook the vegetables for 3–4 minutes, until almost tender, then drain. Return to the pan and gently stir in 1½ cups store-bought tomato sauce into the vegetables. Transfer to an ovenproof dish and sprinkle with 2 slices of slightly stale bread, cubed. Top with 1 cup shredded cheese (such as cheddar cheese or mozzarella) and cook in a preheated oven, at 400°F, for about 20 minutes, until bubbling and crisp. Serve with green salad, if desired.

Red Cabbage and Beet Lentils

Serves 2

2 tablespoons olive or
   vegetable oil
½ small red cabbage, thinly sliced
2 scallions, sliced,
   plus extra to garnish
1 beet, coarsely grated
1 teaspoon ground cumin
1½ cups cooked green lentils
   or rinsed and drained,
   canned green lentils
salt and black pepper
plain or Greek yogurt, to serve

- Heat the oil in a saucepan and cook the red cabbage and scallion over medium heat for about 5 minutes, until just beginning to soften. Stir in the beet, then cover and cook for another 8–10 minutes, stirring occasionally, until the vegetables are tender.

- Sprinkle with the ground cumin and stir over the heat for a minute, then add the lentils and heat until hot. Season to taste, then spoon into 2 warm dishes and serve with a dollop of yogurt and extra sliced scallions.

 Red Cabbage Coleslaw

In a bowl, combine ½ small red cabbage with 1 small shredded beet and 1 small peeled, cored, and shredded Pippin or Red Delicious apple. In a small bowl, whisk 1 tablespoon whole-grain mustard with 1 finely chopped scallion, 2 teaspoons red wine vinegar, and 2 tablespoons olive oil. Pour the dressing over the vegetables and mix really well to coat. Serve with warm whole-wheat pita breads.

 Fruity Braised Red Cabbage

Heat 2 tablespoons olive or vegetable oil in a saucepan and gently cook 1 finely chopped red onion over medium heat for 6–7 minutes, until softened. Add 1 chopped garlic clove and 1 teaspoon ground cumin, then stir in half a shredded red cabbage, 1 peeled and shredded Pippin or Red Delcious apple, and a small handful of raisins. Cook gently for about 15 minutes, stirring frequently, until the vegetables are softened but still have some bite. Season to taste, then stir in 2 teaspoons balsamic vinegar and serve with cooked vegetarian sausages or good-quality link sausages.

Warm Bacon, Tomato, and Lima Bean Salad

Serves 4

3 tablespoons olive or
vegetable oil

6 bacon slices, chopped

2 garlic cloves, chopped

1 teaspoon paprika

3 tomatoes, seeded and diced

2 (15 oz) cans lima beans, rinsed
and drained

2 tablespoons chopped parsley

2 tablespoons lemon juice

- Heat the oil in a large skillet and cook the bacon over medium heat for 6–7 minutes, stirring occasionally, until crisp and browned. Stir in the garlic and paprika for the final minute of cooking, then add the tomatoes, lima beans, parsley, and lemon juice and toss to warm through.

- Spoon into 4 dishes and serve immediately.

 Tomato, Bacon, and Lima Bean Soup Heat the oil in a large saucepan and cook the bacon and 1 chopped onion for 7–8 minutes, until lightly browned. Add 2 chopped garlic cloves and 1 teaspoon paprika for the final minute of cooking. Add 1 (15 oz) can lima beans, rinsed and drained, then 8 chopped sun-dried tomatoes, 2 cups tomato puree or sauce, and 2 cups hot ham or vegetable stock. Season with a generous pinch of pepper, then simmer for about 10 minutes. Use a handheld immersion blender to blend until smooth (alternatively, serve as a chunky soup), then ladle into warm bowls to serve, sprinkled with a pinch of chopped parsley, if desired.

 Tomato, Bacon, and Lima Bean Stew Heat 3 tablespoons olive or vegetable oil in a large saucepan and cook 6 slices of coarsely chopped bacon over medium heat for 4–5 minutes, until golden, then add 1 chopped onion and cook for another 4–5 minutes, until softened. Stir 2 large carrots, peeled and diced, 2 chopped garlic cloves, and 1 teaspoon paprika into the pan and cook for 1–2 minutes, until the garlic is softened. Add 1 (15 oz) can lima beans, rinsed and drained, 1 (14½ oz) can diced tomatoes, and 1 cup hot vegetable stock. Bring to a boil, then cover, reduce the heat, and simmer gently for about 15 minutes, until thickened. Sprinkle with 2 tablespoons chopped cilantro and serve with couscous.

 # Lime and Ginger Chicken Bowl

Serves 2

8 oz chicken breast, sliced
1 cup long-grain rice
2 cups snow peas (optional)
lime wedges, to serve

For the marinade

1 tablespoon vegetable oil
2 tablespoons light soy sauce
1 inch piece of fresh ginger root,
   peeled and grated
1 garlic clove, peeled and grated

For the dressing

1 inch piece of fresh ginger root,
   peeled and grated
grated rind and juice of 2 limes
2 tablespoons light soy sauce
2 tablespoons vegetable oil
1 bunch of cilantro, chopped

- Mix the chicken with the marinade ingredients and let stand in the refrigerator to marinate for about 15 minutes.

- Cook the rice in a large saucepan of lightly salted boiling water according to the package directions, until just tender. Drain well and set aside to cool slightly.

- Meanwhile, combine the dressing ingredients and set aside. Place the snow peas in a small bowl with enough boiling water to cover. Set aside for 2–3 minutes, until they are just tender but still have a slight crunch, then drain and set aside.

- Heat a dry skillet and cook the marinated chicken gently for 10–12 minutes, stirring occasionally, until cooked through but not browned.

- Meanwhile, stir the dressing into the rice. Fold through the cooked chicken and snow peas and spoon into dishes to serve.

 ### Lime and Ginger Chicken Pot Noodle

Divide 5 oz cooked, straight-to-wok noodles between 2 bowls and top with 8 oz (1⅓ cups) cooked chicken, 1 teaspoon peeled and chopped fresh ginger root, 2 sliced scallions, 2 cups shredded snow peas, 1 tablespoon soy sauce, and 2 tablespoons lime juice. Pour 1 cup boiling vegetable stock into each bowl to cover the contents. Cover and set aside for 4–5 minutes, until the noodles are tender. Serve immediately.

 ### Lime and Ginger Chicken

Wrap Mix 8 oz sliced chicken breast with the marinade ingredients given above. Heat a dry skillet and cook the chicken over medium-high heat for 8–10 minutes, until cooked through and lightly browned. Remove from the heat and set aside to cool slightly. Meanwhile, mix 2 tablespoons chopped cilantro with 3 tablespoons mayonnaise and a pinch of black pepper. Spread the mayonnaise over 2 large or 4 small flour tortillas and sprinkle with a small handful of arugula, spinach, or other salad greens. Top with the chicken, then roll up tightly and serve immediately.

30 Beet, Mackerel, and Goat Cheese Lentils

Serves 4

1 cup dried green lentils
3 tablespoons olive oil
2 red onions, finely sliced
½ cup balsamic vinegar
2 cups rinsed and diced,
 cooked beet
2 (3¾ oz) cans mackerel,
 drained and flaked
7 oz firm goat cheese,
 crumbled or diced
chopped chives, to garnish
 (optional)

- Cook the dried lentils a large saucepan of lightly salted boiling water for 15–18 minutes, until tender but still holding their shape. Drain and set aside.

- Meanwhile, heat the oil in a large skillet and cook the onion gently for 12–15 minutes, until soft and lightly browned. Pour the balsamic vinegar over the onion and simmer gently for 2–3 minutes, until the vinegar begins to turn slightly syrupy.

- Remove from the heat and gently stir the lentils into the onion with the beet. Set aside to cool slightly for 4–5 minutes, then spoon into dishes and sprinkle with the flaked mackerel and crumbled goat cheese. Garnish with chopped chives, if desired, to serve.

 Beet Hummus with Mackerel

Coarsely dice 4 store-bought cooked beets, then put in a food processor with 2 tablespoons crème fraîche or plain yogurt, 1 tablespoon horseradish sauce (optional), and 1 tablespoon lemon juice. Process until smooth, then season to taste and spread thickly over toasted whole-wheat pita breads or multigrain toast. Drain and flake the mackerel from 2 (3¾ oz) cans and serve garnished with chives, if desired.

 Beet and Broiled Mackerel Salad

Cook 1 cup dried green lentils in a large saucepan of lightly salted boiling water for 15–18 minutes, until just tender. Drain and cool under cold water. Meanwhile, arrange 4 fresh mackerel fillets on the rack of an aluminum foil-lined broiler pan, skin side up, and drizzle with 2 teaspoons oil. Cook under a broiler preheated to a medium-high setting for 4–5 minutes on each side until just cooked. Place 4 store-bought cooked beets in a bowl with ½ finely chopped red onion (optional) and 1 tablespoon finely chopped chives. Drizzle with 2 tablespoons oil and 1 tablespoon red wine vinegar, then fold through the lentils and spoon onto 4 plates. Serve the salads topped with the coarsely flaked broiled mackerel fillets.

Warm Sardine, Bean, and Potato Salad

Serves 4

1 lb new potatoes, halved or cut into bite-size pieces

2 cups fresh or frozen green beans

¼ cup olive or vegetable oil

1 red onion, thinly sliced

1 (15 oz) can cannellini beans or 1⅔ cups mixed beans, such as cannellini beans, kidney beans, and chickpeas

2 (3¾ oz) cans sardines, drained and flaked

1–2 tablespoons red or white wine or cider vinegar

arugula leaves, to serve (optional)

- Cook the potatoes in a large saucepan of lightly salted boiling water for about 15 minutes or until just tender. Add the green beans for the final 3–5 minutes of cooking—they should be just tender by the time the potatoes are done. Drain and set aside.

- Meanwhile, heat the oil in a skillet and cook the red onion gently for 8–10 minutes, until really tender and lightly browned. Stir in the mixed bean salad and heat gently for 2 minutes, until warm. Remove from the heat and toss with the potatoes and flaked sardines, adding vinegar according to taste. Spoon into 4 dishes and serve immediately with arugula, if desired.

 Sardine and Bean Couscous

Place 1½ cups couscous and 2 tablespoons butter in a bowl, pour in 1½ cups boiling vegetable stock or water, cover, and set aside for 5–8 minutes, until the liquid is absorbed. Meanwhile, pour 1 (15 oz) can cannellini beans (not drained) into a saucepan and warm over medium heat for 2–3 minutes. Remove from the heat and stir in 2 (3¾ oz) cans sardines, drained and flaked, ¼ cup oil, and 1–2 tablespoons red or white wine vinegar. Fluff the couscous, then fold in the sardine mixture with 1 tablespoon harissa.

 Sardine and Bean Casserole

Heat 2 tablespoons olive or vegetable oil in a skillet and cook 1 chopped red onion for 6–7 minutes, until slightly softened. Stir in 1 (14½ oz) can diced tomatoes, ½ cup water, 1 (15 oz) can kidney beans, rinsed and drained, 1 (15 oz) can cannellini beans, rinsed and drained, and ½ teaspoon mixed dried herbs (optional). Cover and simmer gently for 7–8 minutes, until the beans are tender. Meanwhile, cut 1 small French bread into thick slices and spread each slice with 1 teaspoon pesto.

Stir 2 (3¾ oz) cans sardines, drained and flaked, into the beans and transfer all of it into a buttered ovenproof dish. Top with the slices of French bread, pesto side up, and sprinkle with 1 cup grated cheese (such as American or cheddar cheese). Place in a preheated oven, at 425 °F, for 12–15 minutes, until the cheese has melted and is golden. Spoon into dishes and serve with a small arugula salad, if desired.

Spicy Peanut and Beef Wrap

Serves 2

8 oz stir-fry beef strips

2 teaspoon Thai red curry paste

2 tablespoons vegetable oil

2 large soft tortilla wraps

¾ cup bean sprouts

2 small handfuls of shredded
iceberg lettuce

1½ tablespoons roasted peanuts,
coarsely chopped

2 lime quarters (optional)

- Place the beef in a bowl and mix thoroughly with the curry paste so that it is well coated.

- Heat the oil in a skillet and cook the beef over medium heat for 2–3 minutes, until browned but still slightly pink.

- Meanwhile, fill the tortilla wraps with the bean sprouts and shredded lettuce. Top with the spicy beef strips, sprinkle with the chopped peanuts, and squeeze a little lime juice, if using, over the top. Roll up the wraps tightly to serve.

Beef Skewers with Satay Sauce

Mix 8 oz diced beef with 2 teaspoons Thai red curry paste and 1 tablespoon dried coconut. Cut 1 red bell pepper and 1 onion into bite-size pieces and thread onto skewers with the beef. Let marinate. Meanwhile, mix 3 tablespoons chunky peanut butter with 1 teaspoon Thai red curry paste, 1 tablespoon lime juice, and 3 tablespoons dried coconut. Warm gently to melt. Arrange the skewers on a broiler rack. Cook under a medium-high broiler for 8–10 minutes, turning occasionally, until tender. Let rest for 2 minutes. Serve with steamed rice, drizzled with the warm satay sauce and garnished with cilantro.

Beef and Bean Sprouts with

Peanuts Place a skillet over low heat and add a small handful of blanched peanuts. Cook over low heat for 3–4 minutes, until toasted. Transfer to a plate and return the skillet to the heat. Add 2 tablespoons vegetable oil and cook 8 oz stir-fry beef strips over medium-high heat for 1–2 minutes, until browned, then add ¾ cup bean sprouts and cook for 1 minute. Stir in 2 teaspoons Thai red curry paste, 1 cup coconut milk, and 1 cup hot chicken or vegetable stock. Bring to a boil, then simmer gently for 5 minutes. Remove from the heat and stir in 2 tablespoons lime juice. Meanwhile, cook 4 oz flat rice noodles in boiling water according to the package directions, until just tender. Pile the noodles into 2 deep bowls and ladle the aromatic beef over them. Sprinkle with the toasted peanuts and a few chopped cilantro leaves, if desired, to serve.

30 Spaghetti and Meatballs with Spicy Tomato Sauce

Serves 4

8 herb-flavor link sausages or
  20–24 prepared meatballs
2 tablespoons olive or
  vegetable oil
1 onion, chopped or sliced
1 celery stick, trimmed
2 garlic cloves, crushed
½–1 teaspoon dried
  red pepper flakes
2 cups tomato puree or sauce
1 tablespoon ketchup
1 lb whole-wheat spaghetti
salt and black pepper

- If using sausages, squeeze the meat out of the casings and form into about 20 meatballs. Heat the oil in a saucepan and cook the meatballs over medium heat for 6–7 minutes, turning occasionally, until golden. Remove with a slotted spoon and return the pan to the heat.

- Add the onion, celery, and garlic to the pan and cook for 6–7 minutes, until softened and lightly browned, then add the dried red pepper flakes, tomato puree, and ketchup. Season lightly, cover, and simmer for 12–15 minutes, until thickened slightly. Return the meatballs to the pan for the final 7–8 minutes of cooking time, until they are thoroughly cooked, then remove the pan from the heat.

- Meanwhile, cook the spaghetti in a large saucepan of lightly salted boiling water according to the package directions, until just tender. Drain the pasta and pile into 4 warm bowls, then top with the meatballs and sauce to serve.

---

1 Spicy Tomato Meatball Stew

Heat 2 tablespoons olive or vegetable oil in a saucepan and cook 1 finely chopped red onion for 6–7 minutes, until softened. Add 1 lb cooked meatballs to the onion with 2 cups tomato sauce, 1 tablespoon harissa or Tabasco sauce, and 1 (15 oz) can chickpeas, rinsed and drained. Bring to a boil, then simmer for 1–2 minutes, until hot. Serve the meatball stew in bowls with couscous, if desired.

2 Spicy Tomato Meatball Wraps

Place 1 lb ground beef or turkey in a bowl with ¼ cup Mexican spice mix (such as fajita seasoning), 2 finely chopped scallions, 1 crushed garlic clove, and 1 teaspoon dried oregano. Season and mix really well with your hands, then form into 20 meatballs. Heat 2 tablespoons olive or vegetable oil in a skillet and cook the meatballs over medium heat for 12–14 minutes, turning occasionally, until golden and cooked through. Meanwhile, warm 2 cups cooked rice, then divide it among 4 large soft tortilla wraps. Top with 1⅓ cups shredded cheddar cheese and a generous dollop of spicy tomato salsa. Arrange the meatballs over the spicy tomato sauce, then roll up and wrap each one in aluminum foil. Cook in a preheated oven, at 400°F, for 3–4 minutes, until the wraps are soft and warm. Serve from the foil with shredded iceberg lettuce, if desired.

 # Lemon Salmon Nuggets

Serves 2

1 large sweet potato,
  cut into wedges

⅓ cup olive or vegetable oil,
  plus extra for frying

2 tablespoons all-purpose flour

1 egg, beaten

1 cup fresh or ½ cup dried
  bread crumbs

2 teaspoons finely grated
  lemon rind

8 oz salmon or other boneless
  fish fillet, cut into thick,
  chunky strips

salt and black pepper

To serve (optional)

green salad or vegetables

lemon wedges

- Toss the sweet potato wedges in a bowl with 2 tablespoons of the oil and a pinch each of salt and black pepper. Transfer to a baking sheet and bake in a preheated oven, at 400°F, for about 25 minutes, turning occasionally, until tender and browned.

- Meanwhile, place the flour, egg, and bread crumbs in 3 separate dishes. Mix the lemon rind into the bread crumbs. Season the flour with a pinch each of salt and black pepper and dust the pieces of salmon to coat. Dip the fish pieces, one by one, first into the seasoned flour, then into the beaten egg, then into the bread crumbs, turning to coat completely.

- Heat the remaining oil in a large nonstick skillet and cook the fish nuggets for about 3 minutes on each side, until they are golden and crispy and the salmon is flaky. Remove, drain on paper towels and keep warm.

- Serve the nuggets with the potato wedges and green salad or vegetables and lemon wedges, if desired.

 ### Smoked Salmon with Lemon Mayo

Mix 2 tablespoons mayonnaise with 1 teaspoon lemon juice and spread evenly over 4 slices of whole-wheat or multigrain bread. Top each with a small handful of baby spinach, then divide 4 large slices of smoked salmon on top. Season generously with black pepper and serve with a squeeze of lemon juice, if desired.

 ### Broiled Salmon with Mashed

Potatoes Cook 2 large, peeled Yukon gold or russet potatoes, cut into chunks, in a large saucepan of lightly salted boiling water for 12–15 minutes, until tender. Rub 1 teaspoon oil over 2 chunky salmon fillets and place on the rack of an aluminum foil-lined broiler pan. Season with a pinch of black pepper and cook under a broiler preheated to a medium-high setting for 4–6 minutes on each side, or until cooked but still slightly pink in the middle. Drain the potatoes, then return to the pan with 1 heaping tablespoon horseradish sauce, 2 tablespoons butter, and a splash of milk. Mash until smooth, then spoon onto 2 warm plates. Top with the salmon and serve immediately with steamed spinach, if desired, and lemon wedges.

QuickCook
Chilled-Out
TV Dinners

Recipes listed by cooking time

30

20

10

10 Mexican Hot Dogs

Serves 4

2 tablespoons vegetable oil

1 red onion, thinly sliced

1 red bell pepper, thinly sliced

4 teaspoons Mexican spice mix
or medium chili powder

1 tablespoon lemon juice or water

8 cooked frankfurters or
sausages

4–8 hot dog buns, split

creamy coleslaw, to serve
(optional)

- Heat the oil in a large skillet and cook the onion and bell pepper over high heat for 5–6 minutes, until browned.

- Reduce the heat, add the Mexican spice mix, lemon juice or water, and frankfurters to the skillet, and cook for 2–3 minutes, shaking the skillet frequently to cook evenly.

- Arrange the piri piri hot dogs in their hot dog buns and serve immediately with creamy coleslaw.

2 Mexican Sausage and Beans

Cut 6 link pork sausages into 1 inch chunks. Heat 2 tablespoons olive or vegetable oil in a large skillet and cook the sausage pieces over medium heat with 1 finely chopped onion and 1 finely chopped red bell pepper for about 8 minutes, until the vegetables are softened. Add 1 tablespoon Mexican spice mix and cook for another 2 minutes, stirring frequently. Pour 2 cups tomato puree or sauce into the skillet with 2 (15 oz) cans beans (such as kidney beans, navy, or cannellini beans) and simmer gently for 7–8 minutes, until the beans are tender and the sauce is rich and thick. Serve with toast or with baked potatoes for a more substantial meal.

3 Baked Mexican Sausages

Place 8 of your preferred link sausages in a large roasting pan with 1 large onion and 2 red bell peppers that have been cut into thin wedges. Toss with 3 tablespoons vegetable oil, 1 tablespoon lemon juice, and 4 teaspoons Mexican spice mix, then bake in a preheated oven, at 400°F, for 20–25 minutes, turning occasionally, until the sausages are cooked through. Serve with crusty bread and creamy coleslaw.

 # Tuna and Olive Pasta

Serves 2 as a light lunch or snack or 4 as an appetizer

3 tablespoons olive or
   vegetable oil
1 red onion, sliced
2 garlic cloves, chopped
2 (14½ oz) cans diced tomatoes
½ teaspoon dried red pepper
   flakes (optional)
1 lb pasta shapes (such as penne)
1 (5 oz) can chunk tuna in water
   or oil, drained and flaked
¾ cup coarsely chopped, pitted
   ripe black or green olives

- Heat the oil in a large skillet or saucepan and cook the onion over medium heat for 6–7 minutes, until it begins to soften. Add the garlic and cook for another minute. Pour the diced tomatoes into the skillet with the dried red pepper flakes, if using. Simmer gently for 8–10 minutes, until thickened slightly.

- Meanwhile, bring a large saucepan of lightly salted water to a boil and cook the pasta according to the package directions until just tender. Drain and return to the pan. Stir the sauce into the pasta with the tuna and olives and pile into 4 warm dishes to serve.

 ### Tuna and Olive Salad

Lower 4 medium eggs into a saucepan of boiling water and simmer gently for 6–7 minutes. Meanwhile, shred 1 small iceberg lettuce, cut 2 tomatoes into wedges, and flake the drained tuna from 1 (5 oz) can. Arrange the salad on 4 plates and sprinkle with ¾ cup pitted, ripe black or green olives and 3 cups herbed croutons (optional). Cool the eggs under cold running water, then peel. Cut into quarters and arrange on top of each salad. Serve immediately with a French-style vinaigrette.

 ### Tuna and Olive Bean Burgers

Drain 1 (15 oz) can navy beans and place in a bowl. Mash the beans with the back of a fork or a vegetable masher to crush, then add 1 (5 oz) can tuna, drained, ½ cup finely chopped, pitted green olives, ⅔ cup drained corn kernels, 2 finely chopped scallions, 1 medium beaten egg, and 1 tablespoon chopped chives (optional). Mash together really well, then season with a little salt and black pepper and form into 4 large patties. Dust with a little flour or dried bread crumbs and chill for about

15 minutes, until slightly firm. Pan-fry over medium heat in a large skillet for 2–3 minutes on each side, until golden. Arrange on 4 burger buns with your desired fillings (such as a slice of cheddar cheese or American cheese, slices of tomatoes, and a couple of lettuce leaves). Top with ketchup, mayonnaise, or tartar sauce and serve immediately.

1 Quick Garlicky Tomato Lentils

Serves 4

2 tablespoons olive or
   vegetable oil

1 large onion, chopped

2 garlic cloves, chopped

2 cups store-bought
   tomato sauce

1 teaspoon dried oregano or
   mixed herbs (optional)

4 cups cooked green lentils or
   canned lentils, drained

1 cup shredded cheddar cheese,
   or grated Parmesan cheese
   (optional)

crusty bread or toast, to serve
   (optional)

- Heat the oil in a large skillet and cook the onion and garlic over medium heat for 6–7 minutes, stirring frequently, until softened. Add the pasta sauce, dried oregano or mixed herbs, if using, and lentils and heat to simmering point.

- Spoon into bowls. Sprinkle with cheese, if using, and serve immediately with crusty bread or toast, if desired.

---

2 Simple Tomato and Garlic Sauce

for Pasta Heat the oil in a large skillet or saucepan and cook the onion and garlic over medium heat for 6–7 minutes, as above. Pour 2 (14½ oz) cans diced tomatoes into the pan with the dried oregano or mixed herbs, if using. Simmer gently for 10–12 minutes, stirring occasionally, until thickened slightly, then spoon over cooked pasta or baked potatoes. Sprinkle with shredded cheese to serve, if desired.

3 One-Dish Garlicky Tomato Rice

Heat 2 tablespoons olive or vegetable oil in a large saucepan and cook 1 large chopped onion and 1 chopped red, green, or yellow bell pepper for 6–7 minutes, until they begin to soften. Add 2 chopped garlic cloves and cook for another minute, then stir in 1¼ cups long-grain white rice. Add 2 (14½ oz) cans diced tomatoes, 1 teaspoon dried oregano or mixed herbs, 2 cups boiling water, and 1 crumbled vegetable bouillon cube. Stir well to combine, then reduce the heat, cover with a lid, and simmer gently for 18–20 minutes, until the rice is tender and most of the liquid has been absorbed. Spoon into bowls and serve with a hot chili sauce, if desired.

Mushroom and Egg-Fried Rice

Serves 2

2 tablespoons vegetable oil
3 cups chopped mushrooms
2 scallions
1 egg, beaten
2 cups cooked rice
soy sauce, to serve

- Heat the oil in a large skillet and add the mushrooms and scallion. Stir-fry over medium heat for 4–5 minutes, until the mushrooms have softened.

- Increase the heat and add the beaten egg to the skillet. Cook for another 2 minutes, stirring frequently, until the egg is cooked. Stir in the rice and heat until it is really hot, then remove from the heat and spoon the mixture into bowls.

- Serve immediately with soy sauce.

Mushrooms in Black Bean Sauce

Heat 2 tablespoons vegetable oil in a large skillet or wok and add 1 large sliced onion and 1 sliced green bell pepper. Stir-fry over medium-hot heat for 3–4 minutes, until lightly browned. Add 2 cups halved mushrooms and 1 sliced garlic clove (optional) and stir-fry for another 4–5 minutes, until softened and lightly browned. Pour in 1 cup Chiniese black bean or sweet-and-sour stir-fry sauce and simmer gently for 3–4 minutes. Remove from the heat and serve immediately with cooked noodles or rice.

Hoisin Baked Mushrooms with Rice

Arrange 8–10 large flat mushrooms in a large ovenproof dish, stem side up. In a small dish, mix 2 teaspoons peeled and grated fresh ginger root (optional) in a dish with 1 crushed garlic clove, 2 tablespoons vegetable oil, and 3 tablespoons hoisin or Chinese black bean stir-fry sauce. Drizzle the mixture over the mushrooms, then cover with aluminum foil and bake in a preheated oven, at 350°F, for 15–20 minutes, until the mushrooms are softened and aromatic. Meanwhile, rinse 1 cup long-grain white rice under running water and cook in a large saucepan of lightly salted boiling water according to the package directions, until just tender. Drain well and spoon into dishes. Top each bowl of rice with 4–5 mushrooms and drizzle with juices to serve.

STU-CHIL-WAA

Creamy Fish Casserole

Serves 4

1½ cups store-bought cheese-based pasta sauce

1 lb mixed fish (such as salmon, cod, red snapper, and Alaskan pollack), cut into chunks

4 oz frozen peeled shrimp (optional)

1⅓ cups mixed frozen peas and corn kernels

2 tablespoons chopped parsley or chives

2½ cups leftover mashed potatoed

1 cup shredded cheese (such as American or cheddar cheese)

sliced green beans or salad, to serve

- Place the cheese sauce in a saucepan and heat gently until almost bubbling. Stir through the mixed fish for 2–3 minutes, until almost cooked through.

- Stir in the frozen shrimp, if using, with the vegetables and bring to almost boiling point. Remove from the heat and stir through the herbs.

- Scrape the mixture into a medium ovenproof dish, then top evenly with the mashed potatoes and sprinkle with the shredded cheese.

- Bake in a preheated oven, at 400°F, for about 20 minutes, until bubbling and golden. Serve immediately with sliced green beans or salad.

 Creamy Shrimp Spaghetti Cook 1 lb quick-cooking spaghetti in a saucepan of lightly salted boiling water according to the package directions, until just tender. Meanwhile, heat 2 tablespoons butter in a saucepan and add 3 sliced scallions. Cook over medium heat for 2–3 minutes. Add 1¼ cups cream cheese with chives and warm gently to melt. Stir in 8 oz cooked, peeled shrimp and warm gently for 2–3 minutes, until hot. Drain the pasta, return to the pan, and stir in the creamy shrimp. Serve immediately, sprinkled with chopped parsley.

 Creamy Fish with Mashed Potatoes Arrange 4 chunky fish fillets (such as Alaskan pollack, cod, or salmon) in a medium ovenproof dish. Pour 1½ cups warmed store-bought, cheese-based pasta sauce over the top and sprinkle with 1 cup shredded cheese (such as American or cheddar cheese). Bake in a preheated oven, at 400°C, for 15–18 minutes, until the fish is flaky. Meanwhile, cook 6 peeled Yukon gold or russet potatoes in a large saucepan of lightly salted boiling water for 12–15 minutes, until tender. Drain, return to the pan with 4 tablespoons butter, 3 tablespoons milk, and a pinch each of salt and black pepper. Mash with a potato masher until smooth. Serve the baked fish with the mashed potatoed and some sliced green beans.

Steamed Bulgur with Broiled Vegetables

Serves 4

1¾ cups bulgur wheat

2½ cups vegetable stock
or boiling water

2 red or green bell peppers,
cut into bite-size pieces

2 zucchini, cut into
bite-size pieces

1 large onion, cut into
bite-size pieces

3 cups halved mushrooms

olive, vegetable, or flavored oil
(such as chili oil), for drizzling

minty yogurt dip, to serve
(optional)

- Pour the bulgur wheat into a large saucepan and pour the stock or boiling water over the grains. Heat until simmering and simmer gently, covered, for 7 minutes. Set aside until the liquid has been absorbed.

- Meanwhile, thread the pieces of vegetables onto 4 long or 8 short metal skewers, then drizzle with a little oil and arrange on the rack of an aluminum foil-lined broiler pan or a foil-covered baking sheet. Cook under the broiler preheated to a medium-hotsetting for 15–18 minutes, turning occasionally, until the vegetables are just tender and lightly charred.

- Spoon the steamed bulgur into dishes and serve alongside the vegetable skewers. Serve with a dish of minty yogurt dip, if desired.

Vegetable Couscous

Place 1½ cups couscous in a bowl with 2 tablespoons butter and pour in 1¼ cups boiling vegetable stock or water. Cover and set aside for 5–8 minutes, until the liquid has been absorbed and the grains are tender. Meanwhile, finely chop 1 small red onion, peel and shredded 2 carrots, and dice 4 cooked beets. Fold the vegetables into the tender couscous with 2 tablespoons vinaigrette dressing and serve immediately.

Vegetable Bulgur Pilaf

Heat 2 tablespoons vegetable or olive oil in a large, deep skillet and add 1 large chopped onion, 1 chopped red or green bell pepper (optional), and 2 garlic cloves, chopped. Cook over medium heat for 6–7 minutes, until the vegetables begin to soften. Stir in 1¾ cups bulgur wheat until the grains are coated in oil. Stir in 2 cups fresh, frozen, or leftover mixed chopped vegetables or peas. Pour in 2½ cups boiling vegetable stock or boiling water with a bouillon cube, then reduce the heat, cover, and simmer gently for 10–15 minutes, until the liquid has been absorbed and the grains are tender. Spoon into bowls and serve sprinkled with chopped parsley, if desired.

STU-CHIL-NAC

Chunky Spiced Bean Soup

Serves 4

2 tablespoons vegetable
   or olive oil
1 large onion, chopped
1 red bell pepper, chopped
1 red chile, seeded and chopped
2 garlic cloves, chopped (optional)
2 cups rinsed and drained,
   canned mixed beans (such
   as kidney beans, pinto beans,
   and chickpeas)
2 cups tomato puree or sauce
3 cups hot vegetable stock
3 cups mixed chopped frozen
   or leftover vegetables
salt and black pepper
coarsely chopped parsley,
   to serve (optional)

- Heat the oil in a large saucepan and add the onion, bell pepper, chile, and garlic, if using. Cook gently over medium heat for 6–7 minutes, until softened. Stir in the beans, tomato puree, and stock and bring to a boil. Reduce the heat slightly and simmer gently for 12–15 minutes, until thickened slightly.

- Add the vegetables and simmer gently for another 3–4 minutes, until just tender. Season to taste, then ladle into bowls and serve hot, sprinkled with coarsely chopped parsley, if desired.

 Spicy Bean Tostada
Heat a large skillet and toast 4 large, soft flour tortillas for 30–60 seconds on each side, until crisp and lightly browned. Arrange on serving plates and spread 1 (16 oz) can refried beans, warmed, over the tortillas. Sprinkle each tortilla with 1 chopped tomato and 1 chopped scallion. Seed and finely chop 1 large red chile, then sprinkle it over the tostadas. Alternatively, drizzle with a few drops of Tabasco or other hot chili sauce. Serve immediately with shredded iceberg lettuce and sour cream, if desired.

 Spicy Bean Quesadilla
Heat 2 tablespoons vegetable oil in a skillet and cook the onion, bell pepper, and chile as above for 6–7 minutes, until softened. Add 2 cups canned mixed beans, or kidney beans and 1 cup hot vegetable stock and simmer for 4–5 minutes, until slightly softened. Mash the beans, using the back of a fork, then spread the chunky mixture over 4 medium flour tortillas. Sprinkle each with ¼ cup shredded cheese (such as cheddar or Swiss cheese), then top with a second tortilla.

Toast each quesadilla for 30–60 seconds on each side in a large, dry skillet until the tortillas are lightly toasted and the cheese is melting. Serve immediately with shredded iceberg lettuce and a dollop of sour cream, if desired.

STU-CHIL-DEG

Honey-Mustard Sausages with Potato Wedges

Serves 4

2 lb new potatoes,
   cut into wedges
¼ cup vegetable oil
1 teaspoon dried thyme (optional)
12 thin, link pork sausages
2 tablespoons honey
2 tablespoons whole-grain
   mustard
salt and black pepper
green salad and/or coleslaw,
   to serve (optional)

- Toss the potato wedges with 2 tablespoons of the oil, the thyme, and a pinch each of salt and black pepper. Transfer to a large baking sheet and bake in a preheated oven, at 400°F, for about 25 minutes, turning occasionally, until tender and browned.

- While the potatoes are cooking, place the sausages on a small baking sheet or in a roasting pan or ovenproof dish. Drizzle with the remaining oil and cook in the oven for about 20 minutes, turning occasionally, until cooked and golden.

- Meanwhile, mix together the honey and mustard. After 20 minutes, remove the sausages from the oven and pour the honey-mustard mixture over them. Turn to coat, then return to the oven for 4–5 minutes, until sticky.

- Remove the sausages from the oven and cool slightly before serving with the potato wedges and plenty of green salad and/or coleslaw, if desired.

 Honey-Mustard Sausage Roll

In a small bowl, mix 1 teaspoon honey and 2 teaspoons whole-grain mustard with ⅓ cup mayonnaise. Cut open 4 small baguettes or similar crusty bread rolls and spread the mayonnaise thickly over the cut sides. Top with 8 sliced cooked sausages or frankfurters and a small handful of green salad, if desired. Serve immediately.

 Herbed Sausages with Honey-Mustard Dip Arrange 12 thin, link pork sausages on the rack of an aluminum foil-lined broiler pan. Cook under a broiler preheated to a medium setting for 12–18 minutes, turning frequently, until golden brown and cooked through. Meanwhile, place 3 tablespoons honey and 3 tablespoons whole-grain mustard in a small saucepan with ½ teaspoon dried thyme, if desired. Heat gently until the dipping sauce is runny and warm. Pour into a small bowl and serve with the hot sausages.

STU-CHIL-ZAX

Cheese and Onion Potato Waffles

Serves 2

4 frozen potato waffles

2 tablespoons vegetable or
olive oil

4 scallions, sliced

1 teaspoon dried thyme (optional)

1 cup shredded cheese
(such as cheddar or
Monterey jack cheese)

black pepper

green salad, to serve

- Arrange the potato waffles on a broiler rack and cook under a broiler preheated to a medium setting for 6–8 minutes, turning once, or according to the package directions, until hot and browned.

- Meanwhile, heat the oil in a medium skillet and cook the scallions over medium heat for 3–4 minutes, until softened. Stir in the dried thyme and set aside to cool slightly before mixing with the shredded cheese and plenty of black pepper.

- Leaving the waffles on the broiler pan, sprinkle with the cheese mixture, then return the pan to the broiler for another minute, until the cheese has melted. Serve with green salad.

Potato and Onion Omelet

Heat 2 tablespoons olive or vegetable oil in a skillet and add 1 thinly sliced large onion. Cook over a medium heat for 7–8 minutes, stirring occasionally. Slice ½ (14½ oz) drained canned potatoes and add to the skillet with 1 teaspoon dried thyme. Lightly beat 5 eggs, season, and pour into the skillet. Cook gently for 5–6 minutes, until the egg is just firm, then sprinkle with 1 cup shredded American or cheddar cheese. Cook under a broiler preheated to a medium-hot setting for 2–3 minutes, until the cheese is melted and lightly browned. Cut into wedges and serve with green salad.

Potato and Onion Pastry

Pockets Put 1 cup diced, cooked leftover potatoes or drained, canned potatoes in a bowl with 2 finely chopped scallions and 1 cup crumbled cheese (such as feta or a blue cheese). Add ½ teaspoon dried thyme (optional) and a generous pinch of black pepper. Unroll a sheet of store-bought rolled dough pie crust and cut out two 7 inch circles. Spread about 1–2 tablespoons onion chutney (optional) over each circle, keeping the chutney away from the edge. Now divide the cheese-and-potato filling between each pastry and brush a ½ inch border around the edge with a little beaten egg or milk. Fold over the dough to encase the filling, crimping together the edges to seal and create 2 pockets. Arrange on baking sheets, then brush with a little extra milk or beaten egg and bake in a preheated oven, at 400°F, for 15–20 minutes, until golden. Serve warm with green salad or vegetables.

Soy Chicken and Rice Noodles

Serves 2

1 (14 oz) package quick-cooking rice noodles

2 tablespoons soy sauce

1 tablespoon sesame or vegetable oil

½ red chile, seeded and finely sliced or chopped (optional)

1 teaspoon peeled and grated fresh ginger root

1 cup sliced or torn cooked chicken breast

2 scallions, sliced

1 red bell pepper or 2 cups thinly sliced snow peas

- Prepare the noodles according to the package directions. Drain, then cool under running cold water. Drain well and place in a large bowl.

- Whisk together the soy sauce, oil, chile, and ginger and drizzle the mixture over the noodles. Toss really well to coat, then add the remaining ingredients and mix gently to combine. Pile into bowls to serve.

 Soy Noodles with Chicken

Heat 2 tablespoons vegetable oil in a skillet and cook 1 large, thinly sliced chicken breast over medium-high heat for 5–6 minutes, until lightly browned and just cooked through. Add 2 cups sliced snow peas, 2 sliced scallions, a ¾ inch piece of fresh ginger root, peeled and chopped, 2 sliced garlic cloves, and ½ chopped red chile. Stir-fry for 2–3 minutes, until softened, then add 2 (7 oz) pouches precooked stir-fry noodles and cook for 3 minutes, until hot. Pour in 2 tablespoons light soy sauce and 2 tablespoons oyster sauce, toss to coat, and pile into bowls.

 Soy Chicken with Rice

Heat 2 tablespoons vegetable oil in a skillet and cook 4 boned chicken thighs, skin side down, over medium-high heat for 6–8 minutes, until browned and crispy. Turn and cook the other side for 4–6 minutes, until the chicken is cooked through. Remove from the skillet and set aside. Meanwhile, cook 8 oz medium egg noodles in a saucepan of boiling water according to the package directions until tender. Return the skillet that contained the chicken to low heat, add a little more oil if necessary, and add 2 thickly sliced scallions, a ¾ inch piece of fresh ginger root, peeled and chopped, 2 sliced garlic cloves, and half a chopped red chile (optional) to the skillet. Stir-fry gently for 2–3 minutes, until softened, then add 1 large handful of bean sprouts and cook for another 2 minutes until slightly softened. Pour in 3 tablespoons light soy sauce, 1 tablespoon honey, and 2 tablespoons water. Return the chicken to the skillet for 3–4 minutes, until hot and slightly sticky. Serve with steamed rice.

30 Potato, Cauliflower, and Spinach Curry

Serves 4

3 tablespoons vegetable oil

4 Yukon gold or white round potatoes, peeled and cut into bite-size chunks

1 large onion, coarsely chopped

¼ cup medium curry paste

½ small head cauliflower, cut into chunky florets

1¼ cups hot vegetable or chicken stock

1 cup coconut milk

1 cup frozen spinach

To serve

cooked rice or warmed crusty bread

chopped cilantro (optional)

· Heat the oil in a large, deep skillet or saucepan and cook the potatoes and onion over medium heat for 5–6 minutes, stirring occasionally, until the vegetables start to brown and begin to soften. Stir in the curry paste and cook for 1 minute to cook the spices.

· Add the cauliflower to the pan and stir to coat before adding the hot stock and coconut milk. Bring to a boil, then reduce the heat, cover, and simmer gently for about 15 minutes, stirring occasionally, until the potatoes and cauliflower are tender and the sauce has thickened.

· Stir in the frozen spinach and cook for another 2–3 minutes, until the spinach has wilted and the curry is hot. Serve spooned over bowls of rice or with warmed crusty bread and sprinkled with chopped cilantro, if desired.

1 Curried Cauliflower Lentils on Toast

Boil 3 cups cauliflower florets for 5–6 minutes, until just tender, then drain. Meanwhile, heat 2 tablespoons vegetable oil in a large saucepan and cook 1 large chopped onion over medium heat for 6–7 minutes, until almost softened. Stir 2 cups of a mild curry sauce into the onion with 2 cups cooked green lentils or canned green lentils, rinsed and drained, and the cauliflower. Stir over the heat for 1–2 minutes, until hot, then spoon over hot toast to serve.

2 Cauliflower, Chickpea,

and Spinach Curry Heat 2 tablespoons vegetable oil in a large skillet or saucepan and cook 1 finely chopped onion over medium-high heat for 5–6 minutes, until beginning to soften and brown. Stir in 3 tablespoons medium curry paste and cook for 1 minute, then stir in 3 cups cauliflower florets, 6 coarsely chopped tomatoes, 1 (15 oz) can chickpeas, rinsed and drained, and 1¾ cups hot vegetable stock or water. Bring to a boil, then reduce the heat and simmer gently for about 10 minutes, adding a little extra liquid if necessary, until the cauliflower is tender and the sauce has thickened slightly. Stir in 1 (6 oz) package spinach and cook for 1 minute, until the leaves have just wilted, then spoon the curry into bowls and serve immediately with warm crusty bread, if desired.

30 Lazy Bacon, Pea, and Zucchini Risotto

Serves 4

4 tablespoons butter

4 oz bacon, diced

1½ cups risotto rice

½ cup dry white wine (optional)

3¾ cups hot chicken or vegetable stock (add an extra ½ cup if not using wine)

2 zucchini, shredded

1⅓ cups frozen peas, defrosted

1 small bunch of basil, shredded (optional)

salt and black pepper

grated Parmesan cheese, to serve (optional)

- Melt the butter in a large skillet or saucepan and cook the diced bacon over medium heat for 6–7 minutes, until browned. Remove half of the bacon with a slotted spoon and set aside.

- Stir in the risotto rice and pour in the white wine, if using, and hot stock. Bring to a boil, then simmer gently for 15–18 minutes, stirring as often as possible, until the rice is tender and creamy. Stir in the shredded zucchini and defrosted peas for the final 2–3 minutes of cooking time.

- Season, then spoon the risotto into 4 warm bowls. Sprinkle with the reserved bacon and shredded basil, if using. Serve with grated Parmesan cheese, if desired.

 Lazy Pea and Bacon Noodles

Heat 4 tablespoons butter in a large saucepan and cook 8 oz finely chopped bacon over medium-high heat, stirring occasionally, for 4–5 minutes, until lightly golden. Pour in 2½ cups boiling ham, chicken or vegetable stock, 2 tablespoons barbecue sauce, 1⅓ cups frozen peas, and 2 (17 oz) pouches prepared stir-fry noodles. Cover and simmer for 3–4 minutes, until the peas and noodles are tender. Lift out the noodles and pile into bowls, then pour the soup over the noodles to serve.

 Lazy One-Dish Pea and Bacon Pasta

Melt 4 tablespoons butter in a large skillet or saucepan and cook 8 oz chopped bacon for 7–8 minutes, until cooked and golden. Stir 10 oz orzo (or use another small pasta shape, such as macaroni) into the pan, then add 2 cups hot chicken or vegetable stock. Bring to a boil, then reduce the heat and simmer gently for 8–10 minutes or until the pasta is just tender, adding a little more stock or boiling water, if necessary. Stir 1 cup frozen peas into the skillet for the final 4–5 minutes of cooking. Spoon into 4 dishes and serve sprinkled with shredded basil and grated Parmesan cheese, if desired.

Pasta with Chile and Anchovies

Serves 2

8 oz quick-cooking pasta
 (such as thin spaghetti)
2 tablespoons olive oil
½–1 red chile, seeded and
 chopped
6 anchovies, drained and diced
1 tablespoon lemon juice
black pepper

- Cook the pasta in a large saucepan of lightly salted boiling water according to the package directions until just tender. Drain the pasta, reserving 1 tablespoon of the cooking liquid.

- Toss with the remaining ingredients and reserved cooking liquid, then pile into warm bowls to serve.

Spaghetti with Tomatoes and Anchovies

Bring a large saucepan of lightly salted water to a boil and cook 8 oz whole-wheat spaghetti according to the package directions until tender. Meanwhile, warm 3 tablespoons olive oil in a small saucepan and add 1 chopped garlic clove and 1 seeded and chopped red chile. Cook over gentle heat for 2 minutes, until just softened. Remove from the heat and set aside to let the oil to steep. Drain the pasta and return to the pan with 2 tablespoons cooking liquid. Toss immediately with the steeped oil, 1 tablespoon lemon juice, 6 diced anchovies, and 10 halved cherry tomatoes. Spoon into bowls and serve immediately.

Pasta Casserole with Anchovies

Cook 8 oz whole-wheat pasta twists or penne in a saucepan of lightly salted boiling water according to the package directions until tender. Add 3 cups broccoli florets for the final 2–3 minutes of cooking time. Meanwhile, heat 2 tablespoons oil in a skillet and cook 1 finely chopped onion over medium heat for 6–7 minutes, until softened. Add 2 chopped garlic cloves and 1 finely chopped and seeded red chile and cook for another 1–2 minutes, until the onion, garlic, and chile are soft. Add a 1¾ cups store-bought tomato-base pasta sauce and stir for a minute to heat. Drain the pasta and broccoli, then return to the pan and stir in the tomato sauce and 6 drained and chopped anchovy fillets. Season to taste, then transfer to a small ovenproof dish and sprinkle with 3 oz diced mozzarella or ¾ cup shredded cheddar cheese (or similar) and bake in a preheated oven, at 400°F, for about 15 minutes, until bubbling and golden.

 # Tuna Gnocchi Casserole

Serves 4

1 lb potato gnocchi

2 (14½ oz) cans zucchini in tomato sauce

1 (12 oz) can tuna in water or oil, drained

1 cup shredded cheese (such as cheddar cheese, Swiss, or mozzarella)

crusty bread, to serve (optional)

- Bring a large saucepan of water to a boil and cook the gnocchi according to the package directions. Drain well and return to the pan.

- Meanwhile, gently warm the zucchini in tomato sauce in a saucepan with the tuna, then pour the mixture over the gnocchi and stir gently to combine. Transfer to a large, buttered ovenproof dish, then sprinkle with the shredded cheese and cook in a preheated oven, at 425°F, for about 15 minutes, until bubbling and golden. Spoon into dishes and serve with crusty bread, if desired.

 ### Open Toasted Tuna and Cheese

Sandwich Lightly toast 4 large or 8 small slices of whole-wheat bread. Meanwhile, beat 1 egg and add 2 cups shredded cheddar cheese, 2 teaspoons Worcestershire sauce, 1 teaspoon mustard, and 2–3 tablespoons milk or beer, and mix well. Drain 1 (12 oz) can tuna and flake the fish over the toast. Spoon the cheesy topping on top and cook under a broiler preheated to a medium-hot setting for 3–4 minutes, until the cheese is melted and browned. Serve with green salad, if desired.

 ### Cheesy Tuna Pastry Pockets

In a bowl, mix the drained and flaked tuna from 1 (12 oz) can with 2 chopped scallions, 1 cup shredded cheddar cheese, 3 tablespoons mayonnaise, 1 tablespoon lemon juice, and plenty of black pepper. Unroll a sheet of ready-to-bake puff pastry and cut it into 8 equal rectangles. Spoon the cheesy tuna over one half of a pastry rectangle, then brush the edges with a little beaten egg. Fold the other half over the filling, pressing down with your fingers. Using the back of a fork, press along the edges to seal the pastry attractively. Repeat to make 8 tuna pastry pockets, then arrange these on a large baking sheet and bake in a preheated oven, at 400°F, for about 15 minutes, until the pastry is puffed up and browned. Remove from the oven and serve with vegetables or a fresh green salad.

 # Lemon Butter Fried Fish

Serves 2

6 tablespoons butter

2 (6 oz) boneless white fish fillets

2 tablespoons chopped parsley
  or chives

1 teaspoon finely grated
  lemon rind

1 tablespoon lemon juice

salt and black pepper

To serve

cooked rice or mashed potatoes

steamed spinach or broccoli,
  to serve (optional)

- Melt 2 tablespoons of the butter in a small nonstick skillet. Lightly season the fish fillets with a pinch each of salt and black pepper, then cook gently for 4–5 minutes on each side until golden and flaky. Remove the fish from the skillet and set aside somewhere warm to rest.

- Meanwhile, add the remaining butter to the skillet and heat gently until foamy. Stir in the herbs and lemon rind and juice, then remove from the heat.

- Arrange the fish fillets on plates with rice or mashed potatoes and steamed spinach or broccoli, if desired, and serve drizzled with the lemon butter.

 Lemony Fish Pâté on Toast

Drain 1 (5 oz) can of herrings and place the fish in a bowl with 2 tablespoons cream cheese, 1 tablespoon lemon juice, a pinch of finely grated lemon rind, 1 tablespoon finely chopped chives, and a generous pinch of black pepper. Mash with a fork until combined to a coarse pâté. Serve on crusty multigrain bread with baby spinach leaves or arugula and lemon wedges.

 Lemony Baked Fish Packages

Cut 2 large circles out of parchment paper, and 2 more from a sheet of aluminum foil. Place 1 parchment paper circle on top of 1 foil circle, then repeat with the remaining circles. Arrange a generous handful of washed spinach leaves in the center of each layered circle. Place 1 (6 oz) chunky white fish fillet on top of each mound of spinach and top each with 2 tablespoons diced butter. Sprinkle ½ teaspoon finely grated lemon rind, ½ tablespoon chopped parsley or chives, and a pinch each of salt and black pepper over each fillet and finish with a squeeze of lemon juice. Scrunch up the foil to seal the edges, then place on a baking sheet and bake in a preheated oven, at 350°F, for 15–20 minutes or until cooked and flaky. Serve the fish and spinach with new potatoes or rice and drizzled with the lemony butter juices.

STU-CHIL-TAT

1 Minted Potato, Red Onion, and Feta Salad

Serves 2

1 (28 oz) can new potatoes, drained
1 small bunch of mint, chopped
½ small red onion, finely sliced
1 tablespoon lemon juice
⅔ cup diced or crumbled feta cheese

- Place the new potatoes in a large bowl with the mint, red onion, and lemon juice and toss gently to combine.

- Divide the salad between 2 dishes. Sprinkle with the feta cheese and serve.

 Minty Pea, Red Onion, and Feta Omelet with Salad Heat 1 tablespoon olive or vegetable oil in a skillet and cook 1 thinly sliced, small red onion over medium heat for 6–7 minutes, until softened. Meanwhile, cook 1 cup frozen peas in a saucepan of boiling water for 3–4 minutes, until just tender, then drain and add to the skillet of onions with 1 cup sliced, cooked potatoes, 4 lightly beaten eggs, 1 tablespoon chopped mint, and a pinch each of salt and black pepper. Cook gently, without stirring, for 4–5 minutes, until almost set. Sprinkle with ⅔ cup crumbled feta cheese and cook under a broiler preheated to a medium-high setting for 3–5 minutes, until set. Slice into wedges and serve with salad greens.

 Mint, Red Onion, and Feta Rice Salad Cook 1 cup long-grain and wild rice mixture in a saucepan of boiling water according to package directions, until just tender. Cool under running cold water, then drain well. Meanwhile, combine the finely grated rind and juice of 1 lime in a large bowl with 2 tablespoons olive or vegetable oil, half a finely chopped red onion, 1 small bunch of chopped mint, and ½ cup coarsely chopped, pitted ripe black olives (optional). Stir this mixture through the rice with ⅓ cup crumbled feta cheese and ¼ cucumber, seeded and diced, then spoon the salad into 2 dishes and serve sprinkled with another ⅓ cup diced or crumbled feta cheese and lime wedges, if desired.

 # Stove-Top Chorizo Pizza

Serves 2

1 (6½ oz) pizza crust mix
½ cup lukewarm water
1½ tablespoons tomato paste
2 teaspoons ketchup
2 teaspoons olive or vegetable oil
pinch of dried oregano
2 oz thinly sliced chorizo sausage
4 oz mozzarella, sliced
salt and black pepper
2 small handfuls of arugula leaves,
   to serve

- Make up the pizza crust mix by mixing it with the lukewarm water and knead for 4–5 minutes or until smooth. (Alternatively, follow the package directions.) Roll out the dough to make a 12 inch circle and set aside to rest for 8 minutes.

- Heat a large, dry skillet until hot and carefully lower the pizza crust inside. Cook over medium heat for about 10 minutes, turning once, until lightly golden.

- Meanwhile, make the pizza sauce. Mix the tomato paste, ketchup, oil, oregano, and a pinch each of salt and black pepper. Spread thinly over the pizza crust in the skillet and sprinkle with the chorizo and mozzarella. Continue to cook for another 2–3 minutes, then place under a broiler preheated to a medium-hot setting for 1–2 minutes, until melting and bubbling. (If you do not have a broiler, cook the pizza crust for 4–5 minutes, until 1 side is browned. Flip over, top with the sauce and toppings, then cook for 6–7 minutes, until the bottom is browned and the cheese is melting.)

- Cut into slices and serve topped with the arugula leaves.

 Under-the-Broiler Chorizo Pizza

Make up the pizza sauce as above and spread thinly over 2 large, plain tortilla wraps. Sprinkle with the toppings as above, then drizzle with a teaspoon olive oil and place under a broiler preheated to a medium-hot setting for 4–5 minutes, until crisp and melting. Serve in wedges with plenty of arugula salad.

 Oven-Baked Chorizo Pizza

Make up the pizza sauce as above and spread it over 2 store-bought mini pizza crusts. Top with 2 oz thinly sliced chorizo sausage and 4 oz sliced mozzarella. Sprinkle 1 small handful of arugula over each one, then drizzle with a teaspoon olive oil and bake in a preheated oven, at 425°F, for 8–10 minutes, or according to the pizza crust package directions, until melted and lightly browned. Serve with an arugula salad.

Jalepeño Turkey Burgers

Serves 4

1 lb fresh ground turkey

1 tablespoon finely chopped
jalepeño pepper

2 tablespoons finely chopped
cilantro (optional)

3 scallions, finely chopped

1 medium egg, lightly beaten

2 tablespoons vegetable oil

salt and black pepper

To serve

ciabatta-style rolls or crusty rolls

shredded iceberg lettuce
(optional)

spicy salsa (optional)

sour cream (optional)

- Place the ground turkey in a bowl with the jalepeño pepper, cilantro (if using), scallion, and egg, then season with a pinch each of salt and black pepper. Mix well to combine, then shape into 4 patties.

- Heat the oil in a large nonstick skillet over medium heat and pan-fry the patties gently for 4–5 minutes on each side or until cooked through and golden.

- Arrange the burgers on the bread rolls with your desired fillings. Top with the lid and serve immediately.

Jalepeño Turkey Melts

Cut open 4 large bread rolls or ciabatta-style rolls and spread the cut sides with ½ cup spicy salsa (optional). Layer 4 oz wafer-thin sliced turkey over each open roll. Sprinkle 1 teaspoon sliced jalepeño peppers, half a sliced tomato, and half a thinly sliced scallion over each sandwich and top each with 2 cheese slices. Arrange on a baking sheet and cook under a broiler preheated to a medium setting for 2–3 minutes, until the cheese is melted and bubbling. Serve hot with shredded iceberg lettuce.

Jalepeño Turkey Chili

Heat 2 tablespoons vegetable oil in a large skillet or saucepan and cook 1 chopped onion and 1 chopped red bell pepper for 6–7 minutes, until slightly softened. Stir in 1 lb sliced turkey breast meat and cook for 2–3 minutes, stirring frequently, until lightly browned all over. Stir in ⅓ cup Mexican spice mix, 1 (14½ oz) can diced tomatoes, 1 (15 oz) can kidney beans, rinsed and drained, and ½ cup beer or water. Stir to combine, season lightly, then cover and simmer gently for about 15 minutes until rich and thick, stirring occasionally and adding more liquid, if needed. Sprinkle with 2 tablespoons chopped jalepeño peppers and serve piled onto cooked rice with chopped cilantro, if desired.

1 Vegetable Noodle Salad

Serves 2

4 oz quick-cooking rice or
   cellophane noodles

¾ cup bean sprouts

3 cup baby spinach leaves
   or shredded iceberg lettuce

1 carrot, peeled and shredded

½ small red onion, thinly sliced,
   or 2 scallions, sliced

1 tablespoon crushed toasted
   peanuts, to serve (optional)

Dressing

1 tablespoon vegetable oil

1 tablespoon soy sauce

2 tablespoons lime juice

- Prepare the noodles according to the package directions until just tender. Drain through a colander and rinse under cold water to cool. Return the rinsed and drained noodles to the pan.

- While the noodles are cooking, combine the ingredients for the dressing.

- Pour the dressing over the noodles. Add the vegetables and toss gently to combine. Pile into bowls and serve immediately, topped with crushed peanuts, if desired.

 2 Bowl of Vegetable Noodles Heat
2 tablespoons vegetable oil in a wok or skillet and add 1 sliced onion and 1 sliced red bell pepper. Stir-fry for 2–3 minutes, until they begin to soften. Cut 1 small peeled carrot into thin sticks, add to the wok, and stir-fry for 2–3 minutes. Stir in 1 cup bean sprouts and cook for 1 minute, then add 3 cups precooked egg noodles and toss for 1–2 minutes or according to the package directions until hot. Mix in ¾ cup of your preferred Chinese stir-fry sauce. Pile into 2 warm bowls and serve immediately, sprinkled with 1 tablespoon crushed cashew nuts.

 3 Vegetable Soupy Noodles
Heat 2 tablespoons vegetable oil in a saucepan or wok and cook 1 sliced onion and 1 sliced red bell pepper over medium heat for 7–8 minutes, until softened. Add 2 cups sliced mushrooms and 2 sliced garlic cloves and cook for another 3–4 minutes, until tender. Pour in 2 cups hot vegetable stock, 2 tablespoons soy sauce, and 1 star anise (optional). Bring to a boil, reduce the heat, and simmer, covered, for 4–5 minutes to let the flavors to develop. Add 5 oz precooked medium egg noodles to the pan, then remove from the heat and set aside according to the noodle package directions until the noodles are just tender. Pile the noodles into 2 deep bowls or dishes, then remove and discard the star anise and pour the soupy vegetables over the noodles. Sprinkle with coarsely chopped cilantro to serve, if desired.

10 Spicy Pea Pasta

Serves 2

3 tablespoons olive oil
½–1 red chile, seeded and
  finely sliced
2 garlic cloves, chopped
1⅓ cups frozen peas
1 lb quick-cooking pasta
  (such as penne or fusilli)
grated Parmesan cheese,
  to serve (optional)

- Heat the olive oil in a small saucepan and cook the chile and garlic over low heat for 2 minutes, until softened but not browned. Set aside to let the flavors develop.

- Bring a large saucepan of lightly salted water to a boil and cook the pasta according to the package directions, adding the peas for the final 3–4 minutes of the pasta cooking time, until both are just tender. Drain and return to the pan, reserving 2 tablespoons of the cooking liquid.

- Stir the flavored oil into the pasta and peas with the reserved cooking liquid and spoon into 2 warm bowls to serve, sprinkled with grated cheese, if desired.

20 Spicy Pea Soup

Heat 2 tablespoons vegetable oil in a saucepan and cook 1 large finely chopped onion over medium heat for 6–7 minutes. Add ½–1 chopped red chile, 1 tablespoon curry paste, and 1 chopped garlic clove and cook for 2–3 minutes. Pour in 2½ cups hot vegetable stock and boil. Add 2⅔ cups frozen peas, then simmer gently for 3–4 minutes, until tender. Take off the heat and blend, using a handheld immersion blender or food processer (or stir in 1 cup leftover couscous or rice with the peas and eat as a soupy stew). Season and serve drizzled with chili oil.

30 Spicy Pea and Lentil Curry

Rinse ½ cup dried red lentils in plenty of water and cook in a saucepan of lightly salted boiling water for 15–20 minutes, until the lentils are almost tender but are still holding their shape, then drain. Meanwhile, heat 2 tablespoons vegetable oil in a large skillet or saucepan and cook 1 large finely chopped onion over medium heat for 7–8 minutes, to soften. Add 1 thinly sliced garlic clove and 1 seeded and chopped green chile and cook for another 2 minutes, until the onion, garlic, and chile are softened but not browned. Stir in 3 tablespoons mild curry paste and cook for 1 minute. Stir in ½ cup water and ½ cup heavy cream and bring to a boil. Stir in ⅔ cup frozen peas and 1 cup rinsed and drained, canned chickpeas, and simmer gently for 4–5 minutes, until the peas are tender. Stir in the drained lentils and simmer for another 2–3 minutes, until the curry is rich and thick. Serve in bowls with cooked rice or warmed crusty bread, if desired.

30 Sweet-and-Sour Pork

Serves 4

3 tablespoons vegetable oil

12 oz cubed pork

1 large onion, cut into
bite-size pieces

1 red or yellow bell pepper,
cut into bite-size pieces

½ cup ketchup

3 tablespoons packed dark
brown sugar

1 (8 oz) can pineapple chunks
in juice

3 tablespoons cider vinegar

1 tablespoon light soy sauce

cooked rice, to serve

• Heat the oil in a large skillet and cook the pork over medium-high heat for 5–6 minutes, until golden brown all over. Add the onion and bell pepper and cook for another 6–7 minutes, until the vegetables are beginning to soften. Add the ketchup, sugar, pineapple and its juice, vinegar, and soy sauce and bring to a boil, stirring frequently.

• Reduce the heat and simmer gently for about 10–12 minutes, until the sauce is thick and the pork is thoroughly cooked. Serve with cooked rice.

 Sweet-and-Sour Pork Noodles

Prepare 12 oz quick-cooking egg noodles according to the package directions, then drain. Meanwhile, heat 2 tablespoons oil in a wok and cook 12 oz pork stir-fry strips for 2 minutes over high heat. Add 4 scallions cut into 1 inch lengths with 2 cups shredded snow peas or thinly sliced baby corn. Stir-fry for 2 minutes. Add a 1¾ cups Chinese sweet-and-sour sauce. Simmer gently, stirring frequently, for 3–4 minutes, until the pork is cooked thoroughly, then toss through the noodles and serve.

 Sweet Chile Pork Stir-Fry

Heat 3 tablespoons vegetable oil in a large skillet or wok and cook 2 chopped garlic cloves and 1 tablespoon peeled and chopped fresh ginger root (optional) for 1–2 minutes, until softened. Add 12 oz ground pork to the skillet for 6–7 minutes, stirring frequently, until the meat is browned. Add 1½ cups halved baby corn and 1½ cups halved snow peas and stir-fry for another 2–3 minutes, until slightly softened. Stir ⅓ cup sweet chili sauce and about 2 tablespoons light soy sauce into the skillet with 1 lb precooked thick stir-fry noodles prepared according to package directions. Stir for 2–3 minutes, until hot, then pile into bowls to serve.

1 Spaghetti with Garlic and Black Pepper

Serves 2

8 oz quick-cooking spaghetti
3 tablespoons olive oil
2 garlic cloves, chopped
2 tablespoons lemon juice
black pepper
grated Parmesan cheese,
   to serve

- Cook the spaghetti in a large saucepan of lightly salted water according to the package directions until just tender. Drain and return to the pan, reserving 3 tablespoons of the cooking water.

- Meanwhile, heat the oil in a skillet with the garlic and warm gently for 2–3 minutes, until softened but not browned. Pour the flavored oil over the cooked spaghetti with the reserved cooking liquid and lemon juice. Season with black pepper. Pile into warm bowls and serve with grated Parmesan.

2 Garlicky Spaghetti Carbonara

Cook 8 oz spaghetti in a saucepan of lightly salted boiling water according to package directions, until tender. Meanwhile, heat 2 tablespoons oil in a skillet and cook 4 oz chopped bacon for 4–5 minutes over medium heat. Add 2 chopped garlic cloves and cook for 1 minute. Set aside. Beat 1 extra-large egg and 1 egg yolk with ¼ cup single or heavy cream, black pepper, and 3 tablespoons grated Parmesan cheese. Drain the pasta and return to the pan with the bacon and the cream. Stir for a minute over low heat to to warm through and coat in the sauce. Serve with extra cheese.

3 Garlicky Macaroni and Cheese

Cook 8 oz macaroni in a large saucepan of lightly salted boiling water for 8–10 minutes, until tender. Meanwhile, place 3 tablespoons all-purpose flour, 2 tablespoons, butter, and 1 cup milk in a saucepan and heat gently, stirring constantly, until thickened. Simmer gently for 2 minutes, then remove from the heat and stir in ¾ cup shredded American or cheddar cheese. Heat 2 tablespoons olive or vegetable oil in a skillet and cook 8 oz chopped bacon for 4–5 minutes over medium heat. Add 2 chopped garlic cloves and cook for 1 minute. Stir the garlicky bacon into the cheese sauce. Drain the pasta and stir it into the garlicky cheese sauce. Transfer to an ovenproof dish, sprinkle with ¾ cup shredded American or cheddar cheese, and bake in a preheated oven, at 425°F, for about 25 minutes, until bubbling and browned (or cook under a broiler preheated to a medium setting for 3–4 minutes, until the cheese is melted and golden, or just spoon into bowls and serve with extra shredded cheese). Serve with salad.

3. Chorizo and Bean Stew

Serves 4

2 tablespoons olive or
vegetable oil

8 oz chorizo sausage, diced

1 onion, thickly sliced

1 red bell pepper, thickly sliced

2 garlic cloves, chopped or
sliced (optional)

2 (14½ oz) cans diced tomatoes

1 teaspoon dried oregano or
mixed herbs (optional)

2 (15 oz) cans beans (such as
cannellini or lima beans), drained

2 tablespoons chopped parsley
(optional)

salt and black pepper

- Heat the oil in a large saucepan or skillet and cook the chorizo, onion, bell pepper, and garlic for about 10 minutes, until the vegetables are softened.

- Add the tomatoes, herbs, and beans, then cover and simmer gently for 15–18 minutes, until the stew is rich and thick.

- Season to taste, then ladle into bowls and serve sprinkled with chopped parsley, if desired.

---

1. Chorizo and Baked Beans

Heat 2 tablespoons olive or vegetable oil in a large saucepan and add 1 finely chopped onion. Cook over medium heat for 7–8 minutes to soften. Add 4 oz sliced chorizo sausage or frankfurters to the onions for the final minute of cooking. Add 2 (15 oz) cans baked beans in tomato sauce and stir for another 1–2 minutes, until hot. Serve immediately, spooned over hot toast.

2. Chorizo and Beans with Penne

Heat 2 tablespoons olive or vegetable oil and cook 1 finely chopped red onion and 8 oz diced chorizo sausage over medium heat for 7–8 minutes, until the onion has softened. Add 2 chopped garlic cloves for the final 2 minutes of cooking. Pour 2 cups tomato puree or sauce into the pan with 1 teaspoon dried oregano and a pinch each of sugar, salt, and black pepper. Cover and simmer gently for about 10 minutes, until thickened slightly. Stir in 1½ cups rinsed and drained, canned fava beans or lima beans for the final 3–4 minutes of cooking time. Meanwhile, cook 1 lb penne pasta in a large saucepan of salted boiling water according to the package directions until just tender. Drain and serve piled into 4 warm bowls, topped with the chorizo sauce.

Beef and Onion Wraps

Serves 4

2 tablespoons vegetable oil
1 lb beef stir-fry strips
1 red onion, thinly sliced
1 red bell pepper, thinly sliced
¼ cup Mexican spice mix
  (such as fajita seasoning)
4 large or 8 small soft flour
  tortillas

For the filling (optional)

salsa
shredded American, cheddar,
  or Monterey jack cheese
shredded iceberg lettuce

- Heat the oil in a large skillet and cook the beef over high heat for 2–3 minutes, until browned. Add the onion and bell peppers and stir-fry for 2–3 minutes, until the vegetables begin to soften and the beef is just cooked but still slightly pink. Sprinkle with the Mexican spice mix and stir-fry for a minute to cook the spices.

- Divide the beef among the tortillas and top with your chosen fillings, then roll each tortilla tightly and cut in half diagonally to serve.

2 Beef and Crispy Onion Burgers

Heat 2 tablespoons oil in a skillet and add 2 sliced onions. Cook over medium heat for 15–18 minutes, turning occasionally, until crisp and golden. Drain on paper towels. Meanwhile, put 1 lb ground beef in a bowl with 1 teaspoon dried oregano, 1 crushed garlic clove, and seasoning. Add 1 small beaten egg and mix with your hands to form 4 patties. Heat 2 tablespoons oil in a skillet and cook for 3–5 minutes on each side. Serve on burger buns with crispy onions and garnishes (such as American or Swiss cheese slices, pickle slices, shredded lettuce, spicy salsa, or mustard).

3 Beef and Onion Stew

Heat 2 tablespoons olive or vegetable oil in a large nonstick skillet and cook 1 lb beef stir-fry strips over medium-high heat for 2–3 minutes, until browned. Remove with a slotted spoon and set aside. Reduce the heat slightly and add 1 large sliced onion and 2 chopped garlic cloves to the skillet for 6–7 minutes, until softened and lightly browned. Stir in 1 tablespoon all-purpose flour and 1 tablespoon paprika for 1 minute, then add 1 (14½ oz) can diced tomatoes, 1 tablespoon tomato paste, and 1¼ cups hot beef or vegetable stock. Bring to a boil and simmer gently for 15–17 minutes, until rich and thick. Return the beef to the skillet with any juices and stir to heat. Stir in ¼ cup light cream and serve with cooked rice and chopped parsley to garnish, if desired.

QuickCook
Dinner for Friends

Recipes listed by cooking time

30

20

Teriyaki Salmon Noodles

Serves 4

12 oz quick-cooking medium
   egg noodles
3 tablespoons vegetable oil
3 scallions, thickly sliced,
   plus 1 extra, finely sliced,
   to garnish (optional)
1 inch piece of fresh ginger
   root, peeled and cut into
   thin matchsticks
1 (8 oz) jar teriyaki stir-fry sauce
2 (6 oz) cans skinless, boneless
   salmon, drained and flaked

- Cook the noodles in a saucepan of boiling water according to the package directions until just tender. Drain and toss in 1 tablespoon oil to prevent them from sticking.

- Meanwhile, heat the remaining oil in a large skillet set over medium heat and cook the scallions and ginger for 2–3 minutes, until softened and lightly browned. Stir the noodles and the teriyaki sauce into the skillet and toss together to coat.

- Flake the salmon over the noodles and heat gently for 1–2 minutes, until hot. Pile into dishes to serve, garnished with some very finely sliced scallion, if desired.

Teriyaki Salmon Skewers Put 1 lb chunky cubed salmon fillet in a bowl and pour ¼ cup teriyaki sauce over the fish. Mix to thoroughly coat the fish, then marinate in the refrigerator for 5–10 minutes. Thread onto 4 large or 8 small metal skewers. Cook under a broiler preheated to a medium setting for about 8 minutes, turning occasionally, until just cooked through. Serve the skewers on a bed of rice or noodles and stir-fried vegetables, if desired.

Teriyaki Baked Salmon Arrange 4 skinless, boneless chunky salmon fillets in a shallow ovenproof dish and drizzle 1 tablespoon teriyaki marinade over each one. Rub the marinade into the fillets and marinate in the refrigerator for 10 minutes. Cook in a preheated oven, at 375°F, for 12–15 minutes, until just cooked but slightly pink in the center. Set aside to rest for 2–3 minutes. Meanwhile, cook the noodles as above, as well as the scallion and ginger. Toss the noodles with the cooked scallion and ginger until hot, then pile into warm dishes and serve topped with the salmon and any juices.

3 Tomato and Basil Soup

Serves 4

2 tablespoons olive or
   vegetable oil
1 large onion, chopped
2 garlic cloves, chopped
2 cups tomato puree or
   canned diced tomatoes
1 (15 oz) can chickpeas,
   rinsed and drained
2 cups hot vegetable
   or chicken stock
1 small bunch of basil,
   coarsely chopped
salt and black pepper

- Heat the oil in a large saucepan and cook the onion over medium heat for 7–8 minutes, until softened. Add the garlic and cook gently for another 2 minutes, until softened.

- Pour the tomato puree and chickpeas into the pan with the hot stock, then bring to a boil and simmer gently for 15 minutes, until rich and thickened slightly.

- Add the basil leaves, reserving a few for garnish. Season to taste, then blend with a handheld immersion blender until smooth and thick, adding a little extra water for the desired consistency. (Don't worry if you do not have a blender; this soup can be served as a chunky version.)

- Ladle into warm mugs to serve and garnish with the reserved basil leaves.

1 Tomato and Basil Bruschetta

Dice 8 tomatoes and tip into a bowl with 1 small bunch of chopped basil, ½ finely chopped red onion, 2 tablespoons olive oil, and 2 teaspoons red wine vinegar. Season well and stir gently to combine. Toast 8 slices of country-style bread, then rub one side of each slice with a halved garlic clove. Arrange the toasts on serving plates with arugula leaves, if desired, and spoon over the tomato-and-basil topping. Serve immediately.

2 Tomato and Basil Spaghetti

Heat 2 tablespoons vegetable oil in a large saucepan and cook 1 finely chopped onion over medium heat for 7–8 minutes, until softened. Pour 2 cups tomatoe puree or sauce with or without basil into the pan with a pinch each of sugar, salt, and black pepper and bring to a boil. Reduce the heat and simmer gently for 8–10 minutes, until thickened. Meanwhile, cook 1 lb spaghetti in a large saucepan of lightly salted boiling water according to the package directions until just tender. Drain and stir into the tomato sauce with 1 small bunch of coarsely chopped basil leaves. Pile into 4 warm bowls and serve with grated cheese.

30 Mexican Chili Hamburger

Serves 4

3 tablespoons vegetable oil
1 onion, finely chopped
1 red bell pepper, finely chopped
⅓ cup Mexican spice mix
  (such as fajita seasoning)
1 teaspoon dried oregano
1 lb ground beef

To serve

soft tortilla wraps or toasted
  burger buns
shredded cheddar cheese,
  spicy salsa and iceberg lettuce
  (optional)

- Heat 2 tablespoons of the oil in a skillet and cook the onion and red bell pepper over medium heat for 10 minutes, until really soft and browned. Scrape into a large bowl and set aside to cool for 2–3 minutes before adding the remaining ingredients. Mix really well with your hands, then shape into 4 patties.

- Return the skillet to the heat with the remaining oil and cook the burgers over medium heat for 4–5 minutes on each side, until cooked but still juicy.

- Serve the chile beef burgers in folded tortillas or toasted burger buns with fillings, such as shredded cheddar cheese, salsa, and shredded iceberg lettuce, if desired.

 Mexican Bean Tostada

Heat a skillet and lightly toast a large soft tortilla wrap for 1 minute on each side. Push into a deep bowl and repeat with 3 more tortillas. Meanwhile, mix 1 (15 oz) can red kidney beans, rinsed and drained, with 1 small finely chopped red onion, 1 finely chopped red or yellow bell pepper, 1 peeled, pitted, and diced avocado and 1 small bunch chopped cilantro. Drizzle with 2 tablespoons oil and 1 tablespoon lime juice. Season to taste. Drop some shredded iceberg lettuce into each tortilla and divide the beans between them. Serve with shredded cheddar cheese, spicy salsa, and sour cream.

 Mexican Beef Fajitas

Stir 1 (1½ oz) package fajita seasoning into 1 lb beef stir-fry strips and set aside. Heat 2 tablespoons vegetable oil in a large skillet and cook 1 sliced onion and 1 sliced red bell pepper over high heat for 3–4 minutes, stirring occasionally, until lightly charred and slightly softened. Transfer to a bowl and return the skillet to the heat with another 2 tablespoons oil. Add the beef stir-fry strips and cook for 3–4 minutes, turning occasionally, until they are just cooked and browned all over. Return the vegetables to the skillet for a minute, until really hot and sizzling. Serve the sizzling Mexican beef with warm soft tortilla wraps and a choice of extra fillings (such as shredded cheddar cheese, jalepeño slices, shredded iceberg lettuce, spicy salsa, and sour cream).

3⬤ Spiced Lamb Kebab with Couscous

Serves 4

12 oz diced lamb

2 garlic cloves, crushed

1 teaspoon ground cumin

1 teaspoon ground coriander

2 tablespoons finely chopped mint

2 tablespoons olive or
vegetable oil

1 large onion, cut into
bite-size pieces

1 large green bell pepper,
cut into bite-size pieces

2 tomatoes, each cut into
6 wedges

To serve

steamed couscous

minty yogurt dip (optional)

- Place the lamb in a bowl with the garlic, spices, mint, and 1 tablespoon of the oil, then rub really well to coat the meat in the spices. Marinate in the refrigerator for at least 15 minutes.

- Thread the lamb onto 4 long metal skewers, alternating with the onion, green bell pepper, and tomato wedges. Arrange on the rack of an aluminum foil-lined broiler pan, drizzle with the remaining oil, and cook under a hot broiler for 7–10 minutes, turning occasionally, until everything is lightly charred and the lamb is cooked to your liking.

- Serve the kebab skewers with bowls of steamed couscous, and a minty yogurt dip, if desired.

1⬤ Spiced Liver with Couscous

In a bowl, mix 12 oz lamb liver or chicken livers with 1 teaspoon each of ground cumin and coriander, ¼ teaspoon ground cinnamon, ½ teaspoon ground black pepper, and ¼ teaspoon ground cayenne pepper. Drizzle with 1 tablespoon olive or vegetable oil and mix really well to combine. Heat 1 tablespoon oil in a large nonstick skillet and cook the liver for 3–4 minutes, until browned all over and just cooked through, but still juicy.

Spoon the spiced livers over bowls of steamed couscous with shredded iceberg lettuce or red cabbage and drizzle with any juices.

2 Spiced Lamb Burgers with

Couscous Place 1 lb ground lamb in a bowl with 1 teaspoon each of ground cumin and coriander, ¼ teaspoon ground cinnamon, and ½ teaspoon dried mint, 1 teaspoon onion granules, and 2 crushed garlic cloves. Mix well, then shape into 4 patties. Heat 2 tablespoons oil in a skillet and cook the patties for 4–5 minutes on each side, until cooked through, but juicy. Serve the burgers with couscous and coleslaw.

30 Thai Fish Cakes with Dipping Sauce

Serves 4

1 lb boneless fish fillets (such as salmon, cod, or Alaskan pollack), cut into chunks

1–2 tablespoons Thai red curry paste

1 tablespoon Thai fish sauce or lime juice

1 small bunch of cilantro, finely chopped

2 scallions, finely sliced

1 medium egg white, whisked

¼ cup vegetable oil

sweet chili sauce, to serve

• Place the fish in a food processor and pulse until it forms a chunky paste. Scrape into a bowl and mix with the curry paste, fish sauce or lime juice, cilantro, scallions, and egg white until well combined. Use slightly wet hands to form the mixture into about 16 little fish cakes. Arrange on a large plate, cover with plastic wrap, and chill in the refrigerator for about 20 minutes. (Alternatively, if you do not own a food processor, chop the fish as finely as possible and mix with the remaining ingredients, then form into 4 large patties. Chill for 15 minutes.)

• Heat the oil in a large skillet and cook the fish cakes for about 2 minutes on each side (or 3–4 minutes on each side, if cooking 4 larger patties) until cooked through and golden. Drain on paper towels and serve with the sweet chili dipping sauce.

---

1 Thai Shrimp Curry
Heat 2 tablespoons oil in a skillet and cook 3 sliced scallions with 2 chopped garlic cloves for 2–3 minutes. Stir in 2 cups store-bought Thai-style curry sauce and boil. Add 1 lb raw peeled shrimp, then simmer gently for 2–3 minutes or until cooked and pink. Serve spooned over bowls of cooked rice, garnished with chopped cilantro.

2 Thai Red Fish Curry
Heat 2 tablespoons vegetable oil in a skillet or saucepan and add 1 tablespoon Thai red curry paste. Stir over a gentle heat for 1 minute to cook the spices, then pour in 1¾ cups canned coconut milk and 1¼ cups hot chicken or vegetable stock and bring to a boil. Simmer gently for 8–10 minutes to let the flavors to develop, then stir in 1 lb bite-size chunks of white fish (such as Alaskan pollack, red snapper, or cod). Simmer gently for 3–4 minutes, until the fish is just cooked, then stir through 1 tablespoon Thai fish sauce or lime juice (optional). Spoon the mixture over bowls of rice and garnish with freshly chopped cilantro to serve.

Bacon-Wrapped Pesto Chicken

Serves 4

4 skinless chicken breasts

3 tablespoons red or green pesto

1 (4 oz) ball mozzarella, sliced

2 tomatoes, sliced

2 cups young spinach leaves, washed

8 pancetta or bacon slices

new potatoes and green vegetables, or tagliatelle and tomato sauce, to serve

- Slice the chicken breasts almost in half horizontally, then open up and spread the pesto all over both cut sides. Layer the mozzarella, tomatoes, and spinach over the bottom half of each chicken breast, then fold over the top to cover the filling. Wrap each stuffed chicken breast in 2 slices of pancetta or bacon and arrange in an ovenproof dish.

- Cook in a preheated oven, at 400°F, for 20–25 minutes, until cooked through and browned. Pierce the chicken with the tip of a sharp knife to check that the juices run clear, then serve with new potatoes and green vegetables or tagliatelle with a tomato sauce.

 Crispy Bacon and Pesto Pasta Salad

Heat ¼ cup olive oil in a skillet and cook 8 chopped bacon or pancetta slices over medium-high heat for 5–6 minutes, until crisp and browned. Drain on paper towels. Meanwhile, cook 1 lb quick-cooking pasta in a saucepan of lightly salted boiling water according to the package directions until just tender. Drain and cool under running cold water. Mix 3 tablespoons red or green pesto with 3 tablespoons mayonnaise or crème fraîche and 1 tablespoon lemon juice Mix the creamy pesto sauce into the pasta with 12 halved cherry tomatoes, then divide among 4 dishes and serve sprinkled with the bacon.

 Pesto Spaghetti with Bacon Cook

1 lb whole-wheat spaghetti in a saucepan of lightly salted boiling water according to the package directions until just tender. Meanwhile, heat ¼ cup olive oil in a large skillet and cook 8 chopped bacon slices or pancetta slices over medium-high heat for 4–5 minutes, until lightly browned. Add 2 tablespoons pine nuts and 2 chopped garlic cloves to the skillet and cook gently for another 2 minutes, stirring frequently, until lightly browned. Stir 1 (6 oz) package finely chopped, washed spinach leaves into the skillet with 1 tablespoon lemon juice and stir frequently for 2–3 minutes, until the

spinach has wilted. Add 1 small bunch of coarsely chopped basil and remove from the heat. Drain the pasta, reserving 2 tablespoons of the cooking liquid, and return the pasta and reserved liquid to the pan. Scrape the chunky spinach-and-bacon pesto into the spaghetti with 2 tablespoons finely grated Parmesan cheese and toss quickly to combine. Pile into warm bowls and serve immediately with extra grated cheese.

Broiled Ham with Apple and Brie

Serves 4

1 tablespoon olive or vegetable oil

4 (6 oz) thick, cured ham steaks, or 1½ lb cured ham cut into 4 steaks

2 tablespoons applesauce, plus extra to serve (optional)

4 oz Brie, sliced

1 teaspoon dried thyme

green salad, to serve (optional)

- Rub the oil over the ham steaks and arrange on the rack of an aluminum foil-lined broiler pan. Cook under a broiler preheated to a medium-hot setting for 4–5 minutes on each side, until cooked through.

- Spread the applesauce thinly over the broiled ham and top with the sliced Brie and dried thyme. Return to the broiler for another 2–3 minutes, until the cheese has melted and is golden.

- Serve with extra applesauce and a green salad, if desired.

Apple, Brie, and Ham Melts

Cut 1 ciabatta-style loaf in half and split each half across the middle to create 4 pieces. Spread the cut side of each piece with 1 tablespoon applesauce, then layer 2 oz wafer-thin ham on top of each. Divide 5 oz sliced Brie among the ciabatta pieces, then arrange on the rack of an aluminum foil-lined broiler pan and cook under a broiler preheated to a medium setting for 3–4 minutes, until the cheese has melted. Serve with a green salad.

Apple and Brie-Stuffed Pork

Cut a deep slash along the sides of 4 thick, boneless pork cutlets to create a pocket in each one. Stuff each pocket with 1 teaspoon applesauce and a thick slice of Brie, then sprinkle with 1 teaspoon dried thyme and wrap 2 slices of air-dried ham around each cutlet, covering the opening. Heat 2 tablespoons olive or vegetable oil in a skillet and cook the pork chops over medium-high heat for about 2 minutes on each side, until the ham is browned. Transfer the pork chops to an ovenproof dish and pour ½ cup dry hard cider or dry white wine. Place in a preheated oven, at 350°F, for 15–18 minutes, until the pork is cooked through, but still juicy. Remove from the oven and serve with cooked broccoli or green beans and roasted potatoes, if desired.

Poor Man's Pesto with Penne

Serves 4

½ cup pumpkin seeds or walnuts
1 lb whole-wheat penne
3 cups arugula
1 small garlic clove, crushed
½ cup grated Parmesan cheese
⅓ cup olive or vegetable oil
salt and black pepper

- Toast the pumpkin seeds or walnuts in a skillet over low heat for 3–4 minutes, shaking frequently. Transfer the seeds or nuts onto a plate and set aside.

- Cook the penne in a saucepan of lightly salted boiling water for 11 minutes, until tender, then drain.

- Meanwhile, finely chop the cooled seeds or nuts in a food processor with the arugula, garlic, and cheese. Add the oil, pouring it in a steady stream, until thick and almost smooth (or make the pesto using a mortar and pestle, or chop the ingredients by hand as finely as possible, then stir in the oil). Scrape into a bowl, season to taste, and stir into the drained pasta to serve.

Poor Man's Pesto Pasta Salad

Cook 1 lb quick-cooking penne in a saucepan of boiling water according to the package directions until tender. Cool under running cold water, then drain. Meanwhile, make up the Poor Man's Pesto as above (or, alternatively, use ¼ cup store-bought green pesto). Scrape into the pasta with 2 tablespoons lemon juice or balsamic vinegar, 12 halved cherry tomatoes, and a generous pinch of black pepper. Stir well to coat and serve with ⅔ cup crumbled feta cheese, if desired.

Poor Man's Pesto Pasta Casserole

Cook 1 lb whole-wheat penne in a saucepan of salted boiling water according to the package directions until tender. Drain. Meanwhile, make up the pesto as above. Stir in 8 oz mascarpone or cream cheese and 3 diced tomatoes. Stir the sauce into the drained pasta and transfer into a buttered ovenproof dish. Sprinkle with 3 tablespoons grated Parmesan cheese, then cook in a preheated oven, at 400°F, for 15 minutes, until bubbling and browned. Serve with green salad.

Smoked Bacon and Chicken Packages

Serves 4

4 small chicken breasts

4 oz smoked cheese or mozzarella, sliced

1 small bunch of basil (optional)

8 smoked bacon slices

2 tablespoons olive or vegetable oil

1⅓ cups tomato and mascarpone pasta sauce (or similar)

tagliatelle or selection of vegetables, to serve

- Slice the chicken breasts almost in half horizontally, then stuff each pocket with the sliced cheese and 2–3 basil leaves, if using. Wrap the bacon around the chicken breasts to seal in the stuffing.

- Heat the oil in a skillet and cook the chicken over medium heat for 5–6 minutes on each side or until the bacon is golden and the chicken is thoroughly cooked. Pierce the chicken with the tip of a sharp knife to check that the juices run clear, then remove from the skillet and set aside to rest for 2–3 minutes.

- Meanwhile, gently warm the fresh sauce in the same skillet, scraping any sediment from the bottom of the skillet. Serve the chicken packages with cooked tagliatelle or vegetables and the warm sauce.

Smoked Ham and Chicken Tortilla Packages Lay out 4 soft tortilla wraps and arrange 2 slices of wafer-thin cooked chicken breast and 2 oz each of wafer-thin smoked ham and smoked cheese or mozzarella, and ¼ cup drained and sliced roasted peppers in the center of each tortilla. Top each with 2–3 basil leaves (optional) and fold the curved edges of each tortilla into the center 4 times to create a square package. Heat a skillet and toast the packages, 2 at a time, for 1–2 minutes on each side. Serve hot with green salad.

Smoked Ham and Chicken Puff Pastry Packages Roll a sheet of ready-to-bake puff pastry into a large square measuring about 16 inches. Cut into 4 individual squares and spread 2 teaspoons green or red pesto over each square. Arrange 2 slices of wafer-thin cooked chicken breast and 2 oz each of smoked ham and smoked cheese or mozzarella in the center of each square, then top with a small handful of arugula leaves. Bring the corners of 1 square into the center to envelope the filling and create a package. Twist the corners together to seal. Repeat with the remaining squares and arrange the packages on a baking sheet. Brush with a little beaten egg and bake in a preheated oven, at 400°F, for 15–20 minutes, until puffed up and golden. Serve on a bed of salad.

Classic Cheese Fondue

Serves 4

1 garlic clove, peeled and halved

1 cup dry white wine

2 teaspoons vinegar
   or lemon juice

1½ tablespoons cornstarch

¼ cup kirsch, brandy, vodka, or
   dry white wine

1½ lb mixture of cheese
   (such as Swiss, Gruyère,
   and sharp cheddar cheese),
   shredded

selection of dippers, such as
   cubes of crusty bread, raw
   vegetables (carrot and celery
   sticks, broccoli and cauliflower
   florets, halved mushrooms,
   cherry tomatoes), cooked
   sausages, pickles, and new
   potatoes, to serve

- Rub the cut side of the garlic all over the inside of a saucepan, then discard. Pour in the wine and vinegar or lemon juice and bring to a boil. Meanwhile, stir the cornstarch into the kirsch, brandy, vodka, or wine until smooth.

- Reduce the heat slightly so that the wine is simmering gently, then pour the kirsch into the wine in a slow, steady drizzle, stirring constantly, for 1–2 minutes, until thickened slightly.

- Stir in the cheese, a handful at a time, stirring constantly and waiting until the cheese has melted before adding more. Once all of the cheese has been combined and the fondue is smooth and thick, scrape into a warm fondue dish and place on a lit fondue base following manufacturer's directions. (Alternatively, transfer the saucepan directly to the table, placing it on a heatproof mat or board. You may need to reheat the pan gently from time to time as the fondue cools and thickens.)

- Serve the fondue with a selection of dippers.

Quick Cheese Fondue

Warm 3 cups store-bought cheese pasta sauce in a large saucepan and stir in 1¾ cups shredded cheddar cheese until melted. Scrape into a warm fondue pot and serve with a selection of dippers, as above.

Creamy Blue Cheese Fondue

Rub a saucepan with garlic, as above. Pour 1 cup dry white wine or hard cider into the pan and bring to a boil. Stir 1 tablespoon cornstarch into 2 tablespoons wine or hard cider, then pour into the simmering pan in a slow, steady drizzle, stirring constantly until thickened. Add 1 lb coarsely diced, creamy blue cheese (such as Saint Agur, Cambozola, or dolcelatte) with ½ cup heavy cream and stir frequently over low heat until melted. Serve with a selection of dippers, as above.

STU-SUPP-DOC

Flaked Mackerel Salad with Lemon Dressing

Serves 4

2 tablespoons olive oil

1½ cups coarsely sliced, cooked new potatoes

½ (15 oz) can mackerel, drained and flaked

1 (5 oz) package arugula or 4 Boston lettuce, cut into wedges, to serve

For the dressing

¼ cup lemon juice

2 tablespoons horseradish sauce (optional)

⅔ cup sour cream or crème fraîche

salt and black pepper

- Heat the oil in a large skillet and sauté the potatoes for 7–8 minutes, turning occasionally, until crisp and golden.

- Meanwhile, combine the dressing ingredients and season to taste.

- Divide the arugula among 4 plates and flake the mackerel over the top in large chunks. Sprinkle with the sautéed potatoes and drizzle with the creamy lemon dressing to serve.

Lemony Mackerel Spaghetti

Cook 1 lb spaghetti in a saucepan of lightly salted water according to package directions, until tender. Meanwhile, heat ¼ cup olive oil in a small saucepan and add 2 chopped garlic cloves and 4 finely sliced scallions. Cook for 2–3 minutes over low heat. Stir in 8 oz flaked, boneless, and skinless smoked mackerel fillets, 3 tablespoons lemon juice, and black pepper. Remove from the heat. Drain the pasta, return to the pan, and add the lemony mackerel. Toss to coat, then serve immediately.

Lemony Spinach and Mackerel

Casserole Drain and thickly slice 2 (14½ oz) cans new potatoes and put into a large saucepan with 8 oz flaked, boneless, and skinless smoked mackerel, 3 finely sliced scallions (optional), 1¼ cups sour cream, the grated rind and juice of 1 lemon, and 1 cup defrosted spinach. Mix gently and heat over low heat for 3–4 minutes, then transfer to an ovenproof dish and sprinkle with 1 cup shredded cheddar cheese. Bake in a preheated oven, at 400°F, for 20–22 minutes,

until browned and bubbling. Serve with salad greens.

Turkey Tikka Skewers

Serves 4

3 tablespoons tikka masala
  curry paste
2 tablespoons plain yogurt
1 lb diced turkey breast
1 large onion, cut into
  bite-size pieces
1 large green bell pepper,
  cut into bite-size pieces

To serve

cooked long-grain rice
mango chutney (optional)

- In a bowl, mix the curry paste with the yogurt, then add the diced turkey. Mix well to coat, then thread onto 4–8 metal or soaked wooden skewers with the chunks of onion and bell pepper. Arrange on the rack of an aluminum foil-lined broiler pan.

- Cook under a broiler that has been preheated to a medium setting for 12–15 minutes, turning occasionally, until thoroughly cooked and lightly charred.

- Serve hot with cooked rice and mango chutney, if desired.

Tandoori Turkey Cutlets with Rice

Sprinkle 3 tablespoons tandoori spice blend or curry powder over 8 thin turkey cutlets. Heat 2 tablespoons vegetable oil in a large nonstick skillet and cook the turkey cutlets for 2–3 minutes on each side or until cooked through. Meanwhile, heat 4 cups cooked long-grain rice in a skillet with 1 tablespoon oil, stir-frying for 4–5 minutes, until hot. Spoon the hot rice onto warm plates and serve with the tandoori turkey cutlets and mango chutney, if desired.

Turkey Tikka Masala

Heat 2 tablespoons vegetable oil in a large saucepan and cook 1 large coarsely chopped onion and 1 diced green or red bell pepper for 7–8 minutes, until softened. Stir ¼ cup tikka masala curry paste into the pan followed by 1 lb diced turkey breast. Stir to combine and seal the turkey, then add 1 (14½ oz) can diced tomatoes and 1¼ cups water. Bring to a boil, then reduce the heat and simmer gently, uncovered, for 12–15 minutes, until the turkey is thoroughly cooked and the sauce has thickened. Stir ½ cup plain yogurt into the curry before serving with plenty of cooked long-grain rice.

30 Margherita Tart

Serves 4

1 sheet ready-to-bake
  puff pastry

3 tablespoons green or red pesto

16 cherry tomatoes, halved
  (or 2 regular tomatoes, sliced)

4 oz mozzarella cheese,
  torn or sliced

12 pitted green or ripe black olives,
  rinsed and drained (optional)

1 teaspoon dried oregano
  (optional)

2 teaspoons olive oil

green salad, to serve (optional)

- Unroll the sheet of pastry on a lined or lightly greased baking sheet and lightly score a ¾ inch border around the edge.

- Spread the pesto evenly over the pastry, working within the border. Arrange the cherry tomatoes and mozzarella over the pesto, then sprinkle with the olives and oregano, if using.

- Drizzle with the oil and bake in a preheated oven, at 375°F, for 20–25 minutes, until the pastry is crisp and golden. Cut into squares and serve with a green salad, if desired.

10 Margherita Salad

Divide 1 (5 oz) package arugula and 16 halved cherry tomatoes or 2 sliced tomatoes among 4 large plates. Sprinkle with 8 oz mozzarella, torn, and 12 pitted olives (optional), then top with ½ thinly sliced red onion. Make a dressing by placing 2 teaspoons of red or green pesto in a small bowl and adding 1½ tablespoons balsamic vinegar and 3 tablespoons olive oil. Mix well to combine, then drizzle over the salads to serve.

20 Margherita Pizza

Spread 4 individual pizza crusts or 2 small pizza crusts with ⅓ cup pizza sauce, leaving a ½ inch border. Sprinkle with 8 oz sliced mozzarella and 8 halved cherry tomatoes. Top with 12 pitted olives and ½ teaspoon dried oregano, if desired, then drizzle with 2 teaspoons olive oil and bake in a preheated oven, at 400°F, for 12–15 minutes, until crisp and browned. Serve with green salad, if desired.

Barbecue Pork Cutlets with Corn and Rice

Serves 4

2 scallions, thinly sliced,
  plus extra to garnish (optional)
¼ cup barbecue marinade
4 (4 oz) trimmed pork cutlets
1½ cups long-grain rice
8 frozen corncob pieces

- Mix the scallions with the barbecue marinade, then rub the mixture over the pork cutlets. Arrange in a shallow ovenproof dish and marinate in the refrigerator for 10 minutes.

- Cook under a broiler preheated to a medium-hot setting for 6–8 minutes, turning and basting occasionally, or until cooked through but still juicy.

- Meanwhile, cook the rice in a saucepan of lightly salted boiling water according to the package directions, until tender. Drain well.

- Cook the frozen corncob pieces in a separate saucepan of boiling water according to the package directions, until just tender. Drain well.

- Spoon the rice into 4 warm dishes, then top with the pork and any barbecue juices and serve with the corn, garnished with extra scallions, if desired.

 Chinese-Style Barbecue Pork Pot Noodles Heat 2 tablespoons vegetable oil in a skillet and sauté 1 lb stir-fry pork strips for 3–4 minutes, until cooked through. Add 2 cups shredded snow peas and stir-fry for 1 minute, then stir in 2 cups cooked egg noodles. Stir occasionally for 2–3 minutes, until hot, then pour 1 cup hoisin sauce into the skillet. Once hot, pile into bowls and serve.

 Barbecue Pork with Potato Wedges In a bowl, mix together ¼ cup ketchup with 2 crushed garlic cloves, 2 tablespoons honey, 2 tablespoons packed dark brown sugar, 2 teaspoons Worcestershire sauce, 1 tablespoon red wine vinegar, 1 tablespoon dark soy sauce, and 1 tablespoon vegetable oil. (Alternatively, use ⅓ cup barbecue marinade.) Rub the marinade all over 4 (5 oz) lean pork cutlets and marinate in the refrigerator for 10 minutes. Heat 1 tablespoon vegetable oil in a large nonstick skillet and cook the cutlets gently for 12–15 minutes, turning and basting frequently, until cooked through. Meanwhile, cook 1 lb frozen potato wedges according to the package directions until browned. Serve the barbecue pork with the potato wedges and cooked corncobs, if desired.

Creamy Curried Shrimp

Serves 4

4 tablespoons butter

1 small onion, thinly sliced

1 inch piece of fresh ginger root, peeled and finely chopped (optional)

3 tablespoons mild curry paste (such as korma paste)

1 ¾ cups canned coconut milk

12 oz raw or cooked, peeled shrimp

small bunch of cilantro, coarsely chopped

cooked long-grain rice, to serve

- Melt the butter in a large skillet and cook the onion and ginger, if using, for 7–8 minutes over gentle heat (to avoid burning the butter), stirring occasionally, until the onion is soft.

- Stir in the curry paste and cook, stirring, for another 1–2 minutes to cook the spices. Stir in the coconut milk and bring to a boil. Reduce the heat, cover, and simmer gently for 7–8 minutes.

- If using raw shrimp, stir them into the skillet for the final 2–3 minutes of cooking—they should be cooked through and pink. Alternatively, stir through cooked shrimp for the final minute until hot. Remove from the heat and sprinkle with the chopped cilantro, then serve immediately, spooned over cooked rice.

Shrimp and Mango Wraps

Mix 2 tablespoons plain yogurt with 2 tablespoons mayonnaise, 1 teaspoon mild curry powder, 1 tablespoon smooth mango chutney, and 1 teaspoon lemon juice. Season with salt and black pepper, then stir in 10 oz cooked peeled shrimp (or 2 cups sliced cooked chicken). Stir well, then spoon onto 4 large or 8 small soft tortilla wraps and sprinkle with a small bunch of chopped cilantro (optional). Add somme shredded iceberg lettuce and 4–5 cucumber slices cucumber (optional), then wrap tightly and halve to serve.

Aromatic Shrimp Pilaf

Heat 2 tablespoons vegetable oil in a large skillet and cook 1 finely chopped onion, 1 tablespoon peeled and chopped fresh ginger root, and 2 chopped garlic cloves over medium heat for 7–8 minutes, until softened. Stir in 2 tablespoons mild curry paste for 1 minute, then stir 1½ cups long-grain rice into the skillet. Pour in 3 cups hot chicken or vegetable stock and bring to a boil, then reduce the heat, cover, and simmer gently according to the package directions, until the rice is tender and the liquid has been absorbed. Fluff up the rice with a fork, fold through 12 oz cooked, peeled shrimp, then cover and set aside for 2–3 minutes, until the shrimp are hot. Serve sprinkled with chopped cilantro, if desired.

 # One-Pan Roasted Sausages

Serves 4

8 good-quality link sausages

1 onion, cut into wedges

1 lb small new potatoes, halved, or
new potatoes, cut into wedges

2 large carrots, washed and
cut into chunks

2 rosemary sprigs or 1 teaspoon
dried rosemary

3 tablespoons olive or
vegetable oil

salt and black pepper

gravy and crusty warm bread,
to serve (optional)

- Place the sausages in a large roasting pan and add the remaining ingredients. Mix well to coat everything in the oil and seasoning and spread out in the pan in a single layer.

- Roast in a preheated oven, at 400°F, for 20–25 minutes, turning occasionally, until the sausages are cooked and browned and the vegetables are tender.

- Serve with hot gravy and crusty warm bread, if desired.

 One-Pan Sausage Omelet Heat
2 tablespoons vegetable oil in a skillet and add 3 cups drained and sliced, leftover cooked or canned new potatoes, 3 sliced scallions, and 8 oz leftover cooked link sausages, sliced. Toss over medium-high heat for 2 minutes, until hot. Meanwhile, beat 6 eggs in a bowl with a pinch each of salt and black pepper, then pour into the skillet. Stir to combine, then cook gently for 4–5 minutes, until almost set. Sprinkle with 1 cup shredded American or cheddar cheese and slide the skillet under a hot broiler, keeping the handle away from the heat. Broil for 2 minutes, until browned and bubbling. Serve with green salad.

 One-Pan Sausage Casserole
Heat 2 tablespoons olive or vegetable oil in a large saucepan and cook 1 halved and thinly sliced onion and 1 trimmed and finely sliced celery stick over medium heat for 6–7 minutes to soften. Add 2 chopped garlic cloves and 2 teaspoons ground cumin (optional) and cook for another 1–2 minutes, until the garlic is just softened. Stir 1 (14½ oz) can diced tomatoes into the pan with 1 (15 oz) can drained and rinsed chickpeas or navy beans, then bring to a boil and simmer for about 8 minutes, adding 1 (5 oz) package washed spinach for the final minute. Stir in 8 oz cooked, bite-size snack or cocktail sausages and stir for another minute until hot. Spoon into 4 deep bowls and serve with crusty bread and chopped parsley, if desired.

STU-SUPP-ZAF

30 Creamy Mushroom and Chive Risotto

Serves 4

4 tablespoons butter

1 onion, finely chopped

2 garlic cloves, finely chopped

4 cups chopped mushrooms

2 cups risotto rice

½ cup dry white wine (optional)

5 cups hot chicken or vegetable
   stock (add an extra ½ cup
   if not using wine)

3 tablespoons sour cream
   or crème fraîche

2 tablespoons chopped chives

salt and black pepper

grated Parmesan cheese,
   to serve (optional)

- Melt the butter in a saucepan and cook the onion and garlic over medium heat for 4–5 minutes. Add the mushrooms and cook for 2–3 minutes, stirring occasionally. Add the risotto rice and stir for 1 minute. Pour in the white wine, if using, and simmer rapidly for about 1 minute, until the wine is absorbed.

- Add a small ladleful of hot stock. Stir constantly and keep the mixture at a gentle simmer. When the liquid has been absorbed, repeat the process. Continue for about 17 minutes, until all the stock has been absorbed and the rice is tender and creamy, but with texture.

- Stir the sour cream and chives into the risotto, season generously, remove from the heat, cover, and set aside for 2 minutes. Serve sprinkled with grated Parmesan cheese.

 Broiled Mushrooms with Polenta and Chives Arrange 8–12 portobello mushrooms, trimmed, in a shallow ovenproof dish and place 1 tablespoonsof garlic butter on the cut side of each one. Cook under a broiler preheated to a medium setting for about 5–6 minutes, until softened. Meanwhile, bring 3 cups hot chicken or vegetable stock to a boil in a large saucepan. Pour 1½ cups instant polenta into the pan in a slow steady stream, stirring constantly with a wooden spoon, until thickened. Reduce the heat and simmer gently for 2 minutes.

Stir in 4 tablespoons garlic butter and 3 tablespoons finely chopped chives. Spoon into 4 warm dishes, then top with the mushrooms and their juices and serve immediately with grated Parmesan cheese, if desired.

 Creamy Mushroom and Chive Linguine Cook 1 lb linguine in lightly salted boiling water according to package directions, until tender. Meanwhile, heat 2 tablespoons butter with 1 tablespoon oil in a skillet and cook 1 chopped onion for 7–8 minutes. Add 10 oz portbello mushrooms, chopped, with 2 chopped garlic cloves and cook for 3–4 minutes, stirring occasionally. Pour 1¼ cups light cream into the skillet with 3 tablespoons chopped chives. Season with salt and black pepper. Boil, stir in 1 tablespoon lemon juice, then toss through the drained linguine to serve.

20 Breaded Fish with Peas

Serves 4

1 (1 lb) package frozen french fries

2–3 tablespoons all-purpose flour

1 extra-large egg, beaten

⅓ cup dried bread crumbs

4 (4 oz) boneless, skinless
white fish fillets (such as
Alaskan pollack or cod)

¼ cup vegetable oil

2 cups frozen peas

1 tablespoon lemon juice

2 tablespoons crème fraîche
or sour cream (optional)

salt and black pepper

tartar sauce, to serve (optional)

- Arrange the fries on a baking sheet and cook in a preheated oven according to the package directions until browned. Meanwhile, place the flour, egg, and bread crumbs in 3 separate shallow dishes. Season the flour. Dust each fish fillet in flour, then dip into the beaten egg, turning to coat. Now turn in the bread crumbs to coat.

- Heat the oil in a skillet and pan-fry the fish over medium heat for 3–4 minutes on each side, until the coating is golden and crunchy and the fish is cooked through.

- Meanwhile, cook the peas in a saucepan of boiling water for 3–5 minutes, until tender. Remove from the heat, drain, and mash with the lemon juice, crème fraîche, if using, salt and black pepper (or put the peas, lemon juice and crème fraîche into a food processor and pulse until mushy). Serve the crispy breaded fish with the french fries, peas, lemon wedges, and tartar sauce, if desired.

 **Fish Sticks
with Peas**

Cook 8–12 fish sticks under a broiler preheated to a medium-hot setting for about 8 minutes, turning occasionally. Meanwhile, boil 3 cups frozen peas for 3–5 minutes. Drain and return to the pan. Add 4 tablespoons butter, salt and black pepper, and 1 tablespoon mint sauce or 1 teaspoon finely chopped mint and stir. Serve topped with the broiled fish sticks with tartar sauce or ketchup and buttered whole-wheat bread.

 **Herb-Crusted
Fish with Mashed
Potatoes** In a bowl, combine 1½ cups fresh bread crumbs with 1 teaspoon finely grated lemon rind (optional), 2 tablespoons finely chopped parsley, 1 tablespoon finely chopped chives, and a pinch each of salt and black pepper. Rub a little oil over the fish fillets and press them into the bread crumb mixture to coat lightly. Arrange in an ovenproof dish or baking sheet and top with the remaining bread crumb mixture. Place

in a preheated oven, at 400°F, for 15–20 minutes or until the crust is browned and the fish is flaky. Meanwhile, cook 6 Yukon gold or russet potatoes, peeled and diced, in a saucepan of boiling water for 12–15 minutes, until tender. Drain and mash with 4 tablespoons butter and a splash of milk. Season to taste, spoon onto 4 warm plates, and serve with the fish and some cooked peas, if desired.

Green Curry Noodle Soup

Serves 4

1 cup coconut milk

1–2 tablespoons Thai green
curry paste

3¾ cups hot chicken or
vegetable stock

2 tablespoons Thai fish sauce
or lime juice

3 cups sliced snow peas or
fine green beans

2 cups cooked medium noodles

- Pour the coconut milk into a large saucepan and bring to a boil. Stir in the curry paste and simmer for 1–2 minutes before adding the hot chicken or vegetable stock and fish sauce or lime juice.

- Simmer gently for 5 minutes, then stir in the snow peas or green beans and noodles. Cook for 3–4 minutes, until just tender, then ladle into bowls and serve immediately.

Green Vegetable Curry

Heat 3 tablespoons vegetable oil in a skillet and add 1 diced eggplant and 1 sliced onion. Cook over medium-high heat for 5 minutes, stirring frequently, until lightly browned and beginning to soften. Reduce the heat and stir in 2 tablespoons Thai green curry paste, 1¾ cups canned coconut milk, and 1¼ cups hot chicken or vegetable stock. Bring to a boil, simmer gently for 5 minutes, then add 1½ cups green beans and 3 cups broccoli florets and cook for another 6–7 minutes, until tender. Stir in 1 tablespoon Thai fish sauce or lime juice and serve over bowls of cooked rice, garnished with cilantro, if desired.

Sweet Potato and Green Bean Curry

Heat 2 tablespoons vegetable oil in a large skillet or saucepan and add 1 coarsely chopped onion, 1 large peeled and diced sweet potato, and 1 diced eggplant. Cook over medium heat for 7–8 minutes, stirring frequently, until the onion is softened. Add a 1 inch piece of fresh ginger root, peeled and chopped, and 2 chopped garlic cloves and cook for another 2–3 minutes, until softened. Stir in 2 tablespoons Thai red curry paste, 1¾ cups canned coconut milk, and 1¾ cups hot vegetable stock and bring to a boil. Reduce the heat and simmer gently for 7–8 minutes to let the flavors develop. Add 1½ cups green beans and 1 thinly sliced red bell pepper, then simmer for another 7–8 minutes, until all the vegetables are tender. Stir in 1 tablespoon Thai fish sauce or lime juice, then spoon over bowls of cooked rice and garnish with cilantro, if desired, to serve.

30 Roasted Red Peppers with Mozzarella and Couscous

Serves 4

4 large red bell peppers, tops
  removed, cored (but left whole)
2 garlic cloves, sliced
2 (4 oz) balls mozzarella, halved
1 teaspoon dried red pepper
  flakes (optional)
12 cherry tomatoes
2 tablespoons olive or
  vegetable oil
1½ cups seasoned couscous mix
2 tablespoons butter
1¼ cups boiling vegetable or
  chicken stock
arugula, to serve (optional)

- Arrange the cored red bell peppers in a shallow ovenproof dish and stuff each one with a few slices of garlic, ½ a ball of mozzarella, a pinch of dried red pepper flakes, if using, and 3 cherry tomatoes. Drizzle with the oil and roast in a preheated oven, at 400°F, for 20–25 minutes, until softened.

- Meanwhile, place the couscous in a bowl with the butter and pour over the boiling stock. Cover and set aside for 6–8 minutes, until the liquid has been absorbed and the grains are tender. Fluff with a fork and spoon onto serving plates. Top with a roasted stuffed pepper and serve with the arugula, if using.

 Quick Bell Pepper and Mozzarella Salad Arrange 4 quartered bell peppers on the rack of an aluminum foil-lined broiler pan, skin side up, and drizzle with 2 tablespoons vegetable oil. Cook under a broiler preheated to hot for 6–7 minutes, until softened and lightly charred. Cool slightly, then slice thickly. Spoon 4 cups store-bought couscous salad into 4 dishes and top each one with a small handful of arugula. Tear 2 (4 oz) balls of mozzarella and sprinkle on top of the arugula. Top with the sliced roasted peppers and serve with a drizzle each of olive oil and balsamic vinegar.

 Broiled Pepper and Cheese Couscous Arrange 4 halved and cored red or yellow bell peppers, cut side up, on the rack of an aluminum foil-lined broiler pan and divide 8 oz drained mini mozzarella balls or diced mozzarella among them. Top each half with a pinch each of dried red pepper flakes and chopped garlic. Drizzle 2 tablespoons vegetable oil over the peppers and cook under a broiler preheated to a medium-low setting for 8–10 minutes or until the cheese is melting and lightly charred. Meanwhile, cook the couscous as above. Spoon onto serving plates and serve topped with the peppers.

Gingery Broiled Tofu with Noodles

Serves 4

2 tablespoons vegetable oil

1 (1 lb) package stir-fry vegetables

1 (1 lb) package fresh noodles

14 oz firm tofu, thickly sliced

For the marinade

1 inch piece of fresh ginger root, peeled and grated

2 large garlic cloves, crushed

3 tablespoons dark soy sauce

3 tablespoons honey

- Heat the oil in a wok or skillet and stir-fry the vegetables for 3–4 minutes. Add the noodles and toss for another 3–4 minutes.

- Meanwhile, mix together the ginger, garlic, soy, and honey. Add the sliced tofu and turn gently in the marinade to coat. Reserve the remaining marinade. Arrange the tofu on an aluminum foil-lined baking sheet and cook under a broiler preheated to a medium setting for about 4 minutes, carefully turning once, until golden.

- Remove the noodles from the heat, drizzle with the remaining marinade, and serve topped with the broiled tofu.

Gingery Tofu Stir-Fry

Heat 2 tablespoons oil in a skillet or wok and stir-fry 8 oz marinated tofu pieces for 3–4 minutes. Remove and set aside. Add 1 (1 lb) package stir-fry vegetables to the skillet and cook for 3–4 minutes, until just tender. Add a 1 inch piece peeled and chopped fresh ginger root and 2 chopped garlic cloves and stir-fry for 1 minute. Meanwhile, mix 3 tablespoons light soy sauce with 2 tablespoons honey, then remove the skillet from the heat, pour the sauce over the contents, and return the tofu to the skillet. Toss to coat and serve with 4 cups prepared egg-fried rice.

Ginger Marinated Tofu and Vegetable

Packages In a bowl, mix ¼ cup light soy sauce with 2 tablespoons sesame or vegetable oil, 2 tablespoons honey, 1 tablespoon peeled and grated fresh ginger root, 2 crushed garlic cloves, and 3 finely sliced scallions. Thickly slice 1¾ lb firm tofu and toss gently in the marinade to coat. Set aside for 10 minutes. Meanwhile, cut 4 large circles from parchment paper and 4 large circles from aluminum foil. Lay each paper circle on top of a foil one. Divide 1 (1 lb) package stir-fry vegetables among the circles. Top the

vegetables with slices of marinated tofu, then drizzle with the remaining marinade. Bring up the sides of the foil-and-paper lining and scrunch together the edges to seal. Arrange on a large baking sheet and place in a preheated oven, at 400°F, for 12–15 minutes, until the vegetables are just tender. Place the packages directly onto 4 warm plates to serve.

Vegetable Curry with Rice

Serves 4

2 tablespoons vegetable oil

1 onion, coarsely chopped

1 (1 lb) package mixed chopped vegetables (such as carrots, potato, cauliflower, and broccoli)

2 garlic cloves, chopped

1 inch piece of fresh ginger root, peeled and chopped

¼ cup medium-hot curry paste

1 (14½ oz) can diced tomatoes

1¾ cups hot vegetable stock

cooked rice, to serve

- Heat the oil in a large skillet and cook the onion and mixed vegetables over medium heat for about 10 minutes, stirring frequently, until lightly browned and beginning to soften. Stir in the garlic and ginger for another 2 minutes, then add the curry paste and stir over the heat for 1 minute to cook the spices.

- Pour in the diced tomatoes and vegetable stock, then bring to a boil, reduce the heat, and simmer gently for about 15 minutes, until the curry has thickened slightly and the vegetables are tender. Serve spooned over cooked rice.

 Vegetable Rice with Curry Sauce

Heat 2 tablespoons oil in a saucepan and cook 4 cups cooked rice for 3–4 minutes, until piping hot. Stir in 2 (15 oz) cans mixed vegetables, drained, or 4 cups cooked, diced mixed vegetables, and stir into the rice for 2–3 minutes, until hot. Heat 2 cups store-bought curry sauce in a small saucepan, stirring occasionally, for 2–3 minutes, until almost boiling. Remove from the heat. Spoon the vegetable rice into warm bowls and serve with the hot curry sauce and crusty warm bread, if desired.

 Curried Vegetable and Rice Bowl

Heat 2 tablespoons oil in a large skillet and cook 1 chopped onion and 1 chopped bell pepper over medium-high heat for 3–4 minutes, until lightly browned and beginning to soften. Add 2 chopped garlic cloves and 1 tablespoon peeled and chopped fresh ginger root and cook for 1 minute, then add 3 tablespoons hot curry paste and cook for 1 minute. Pour 1 (14½ oz) can diced tomatoes into the skillet with 2 teaspoons wine vinegar and 1 cup hot vegetable stock or water. Bring to a boil, then reduce the heat and simmer gently for 6–7 minutes. Stir in 1 (12 oz) package frozen mixed vegetables and simmer gently for another 5–6 minutes, until just tender. Spoon over bowls of hot rice to serve.

 Sardine and Potato Salad

Serves 4

3 tablespoons mayonnaise

2 tablespoons tartar sauce

2 teaspoons lemon juice

2 tablespoons chopped chives
or parsley (optional)

3 cups diced, cooked potatoes

2 (3¾ oz) cans sardines,
drained and flaked

salt and black pepper

- In a large bowl, mix the mayonnaise, tartar sauce, lemon juice, and chopped herbs and season with a pinch each of salt and black pepper.

- Fold through the potatoes and flaked sardines and divide among serving plates.

 Sardine Linguine
Cook 1 lb linguine or spaghetti in a large saucepan of lightly salted boiling water according to package directions, until tender. Meanwhile, heat 3 tablespoons olive oil in a skillet and gently cook 2 chopped garlic cloves and 1 seeded and finely chopped red chile for 2–3 minutes. Remove from the heat and stir in the grated rind and juice of 1 lemon, 1 small bunch of chopped parsley, and 2 (3¾ oz) cans sardines in tomato sauce (or use canned crab, tuna, or salmon). Season to taste. Drain the pasta, return it to the pan, and add the sardine mixture to the pasta. Toss briefly over medium heat, then serve.

 Mixed Fish Casserole
Heat 3 cups tomato sauce in a large saucepan. Add 12 oz mixed fish chunks (such of salmon, red snapper, tilapia, and Alaskan pollack) and simmer gently for 5–8 minutes, until the fish is just cooked and flaky. Flake in 1 (3¾ oz) can sardines in tomato sauce and 8 oz cooked peeled shrimp, then transfer to a shallow ovenproof dish. In a small bowl, mix 1½ cups fresh bread crumbs with 2 tablespoons finely grated Parmesan cheese (optional), 2 tablespoons finely chopped parsley or chives (optional), and 1 tablespoon olive oil. Mix well to coat, then sprinkle it over the fish and bake in a preheated oven, at 375°F, for about 15 minutes, until browned and crispy. Serve immediately with your preferred vegetables, if desired.

QuickCook

Sweet Fix

Recipes listed by cooking time

30

20

10

30 Banana and Caramel Chocolate Muffins

Serves 6

1¾ cups all-puprose flour, sifted

1¾ cups baking powder

2 tablespoons unsweetened
cocoa powder, sifted

½ cup granulated sugar

½ cup semisweet chocolate chips

2 eggs

2 small ripe bananas, mashed

¼ cup vegetable oil

½ cup plain yogurt

warmed dulce de leche
(caramel sauce), to serve

• In a bowl, mix together the flour, baking powder, cocoa powder, granulated sugar, and ¼ cup of the chocolate chips.

• Combine the eggs, bananas, oil, and yogurt in a bowl, then pour the wet ingredients into the dry and mix to barely combine. Divide the batter among the cups of a greased or paper cup-lined, 12-cup muffin pan and sprinkle with the remaining chocolate chips.

• Bake in the preheated oven, at 350°F, for 18–22 minutes, until risen and firm to the touch. Cool slightly on wire racks and serve warm, drizzled with warm dulce de leche.

 1 Banana and Caramel Chocolate Sundaes Crumble 12 chocolate cream sandwich cookies (such as Oreos) into the bottom of 6 sundae glasses and drizzle 1 tablespoon caramel sauce over each one. Slice 3 large, ripe but firm bananas and sprinkle them over the caramel sauce. Top each sundae with 2 scoops of ice cream and finish with a squirt of whipped cream. Drizzle with a little extra sauce to serve, if desired.

 2 Boozy Banana Chocolate Trifle Thickly slice 3 large store-bought (or leftover homemade) chocolate muffins (slightly stale is fine) and arrange the slices across the bottom of a large glass bowl or trifle dish. Drizzle with ⅓ cup Irish cream liqueur (such as Baileys) and set aside to soak. Meanwhile, slice 3 large, ripe but firm bananas and whip 1 cup heavy cream to soft peaks. Sprinkle the bananas over the muffins, drizzle with ¼ cup dulce de leche (caramel sauce), and top with the softly whipped cream. Sprinkle with a mixture of dried banana and chocolate chips to decorate.

10 Mixed Dried Fruit Compote with Ice Cream

Serves 4–6

2 cups mixed chunky dried fruit, such as apricots, prunes, and dates

1½ cups orange juice

1 vanilla bean, split

8–12 scoops vanilla ice cream

· Place the dried fruits in a small saucepan with the orange juice and vanilla bean and simmer gently for 6–7 minutes, stirring frequently, until the fruits swell and have softened.

· Scrape into a bowl and set aside to cool slightly. Meanwhile, arrange the ice cream among 4–6 bowls, then spoon the warm dried fruit compote with any juices over the ice cream before serving.

2 Mixed Dried Fruit Scones

Place 2⅓ cups all-purpose flour and 2 teaspoons baking powder in a bowl and rub in 6 tablespoons softened butter until the mixture resembles bread crumbs. Stir in ½ cup mixed dried fruit and 2 tablespoons granulated sugar. Combine ½ cup milk with 1 extra-large lightly beaten egg, then pour into the bowl and mix to a soft dough. Transfer to a lightly floured surface and gently flatten the dough to a thickness of about ¾ inch. Stamp out about 12 scones, using a 2 inch cutter, then arrange on a lightly greased baking sheet and brush lightly with a little milk. Bake in a preheated oven, at 400°F, for about 12 minutes, until risen and golden. Transfer to wire racks to cool slightly. Makes about 12 scones.

3 Mixed Dried Fruit Rock Biscuits

Sift 2 cups all-purpose flour into a large bowl with 2 teaspoons baking powder and 1 teaspoon ground cinnamon (optional). Rub 1 stick softened butter into the flour until the mixture resembles bread crumbs, then stir in 2 teaspoons finely grated orange rind, 1 cup dried mixed fruit, and ½ cup granulated sugar. Add 1 extra-large beaten egg and 1 egg yolk, plus 1–2 tablespoons milk to bind to a soft dough. Arrange 8–10 mounds of the dough on a baking sheet lined with parchment paper and sprinkle with granulated or raw sugar. Bake in a preheated oven, at 375°F, for 20 minutes or until firm and golden. Let cool on wire racks.

Vanilla and Raspberry Cupcakes

Serves 4–6

1 stick butter or margarine, softened

1 cup all-purpose flour

1 teaspoon baking powder

½ cup granulated sugar

2 eggs

1 teaspoon vanilla extract

12 teaspoons raspberry preserves, to serve

- In a bowl, beat together the butter, flour, baking powder, sugar, eggs, and vanilla extract until really smooth, pale and creamy. Divide the batter among the cups of a greased or paper cup-lined, 12-cup muffin pan.

- Bake in a preheated oven, at 350°F, for 12–14 minutes, until risen, golden, and firm to the touch—a wooden toothpick inserted into the cakes should come out clean.

- Cool on a wire rack and serve each cake topped with a teaspoon of raspberry preserves.

Vanilla and Raspberry Trifle

Slice 1 raspberry jelly roll and arrange over the bottom of a large glass bowl. Stir 1 teaspoon vanilla extract into 3 tablespoons cassis, peach schnapps, or cranberry juice and drizzle the mixture over the cake. Pour the contents of 1 (12 oz) can black cherry filling over the cake, followed by 1 cup prepared vanilla pudding. Shake a pressurized can of fresh cream and squirt several dollops onto the top of the trifle. Serve sprinkled with chocolate curls or a few fresh raspberries.

Vanilla and Raspberry Cake

In a large bowl, beat 3 eggs and 1 teaspoon vanilla extract with ¾ cup granulated sugar, 1⅓ cups all-purpose flour, 1 teaspoon baking powder, and 1½ sticks softened butter or margarine until pale and creamy. Divide the batter between two 8 inch cake pans (first line the bottoms with parchment paper). Bake in a preheated oven, at 350°F, for about 20 minutes, until risen and golden. Remove from the pans, peel away the paper and cool on a wire rack before sandwiching together using 4–5 tablespoons raspberry preserves, or your favorite jam or preserves. Dredge the top with a sprinkling of granulated sugar and serve as fresh as possible, cut into wedges.

Golden Pineapple with Rice Pudding

Serves 4–6

2 tablespoons butter

2 tablespoons granulated sugar

1 (15 oz) can pineapple slices in juice, drained

warm or chilled store-bought rice pudding, to serve

- To caramelize the pineapple, melt the butter in a large skillet and sprinkle the sugar over both sides of the pineapple slices to coat. Add the pineapple slices to the skillet and sauté gently for 2–3 minutes on each side, until sticky and golden.

- Cool slightly, then serve with dollops of warm or chilled rice pudding.

Pineapple Baked Rice Pudding

Spoon 3 cups store-bought rice pudding into a buttered ovenproof dish. Sprinkle with 1 (15 oz) can pineapple chunks in juice, drained. Sprinkle with 2 tablespoons granulated sugar and bake in a preheated oven, at 350°F, for 10–15 minutes, until bubbling. Serve warm with ice cream, if desired.

Coconut Rice Pudding with Pineapple Place ½ cup short-grain rice in a saucepan with 1¾ cups canned coconut milk, 1¾ cups milk, ¼ cup firmly packed light brown sugar, and 2 tablespoons butter. Put over the heat and bring to a boil, then reduce the heat and simmer for about 25 minutes, stirring frequently, until the rice is creamy and tender. Meanwhile, caramelize the pineapple as above. Spoon the coconut rice pudding into bowls and serve with the golden pineapple.

30 Chocolate Orange Cheesecake

Serves 6

2 cups crushed chocolate-coated
   graham crackers or cookies
1 stick butter, melted
1¼ cups cream cheese
   or mascarpone cheese
3 tablespoons chocolate spread
2 teaspoons finely grated
   orange rind
⅓ cup granulated sugar
grated orange-flavored
   chocolate, to decorate

- Combine the crushed cookies with the melted butter and mix really well to coat. Press the mixture into a plastic wrap-lined 9 inch tart or cake pan and chill in the freezer or refrigerator while you are making the filling.

- Beat the cream cheese or mascarpone cheese with the chocolate spread, orange rind, and granulated sugar until thick and smooth. Spoon the mixture on top of the cookie crust and smooth down evenly. Return to the freezer or refrigerator for at least 20 minutes or until required, then remove and decorate with grated orange-flavored chocolate to serve.

 1 Chocolate Orange Milk Shake

Place 4 scoops of chocolate ice cream in the pitcher of a blender with 3 cups milk, 2 tablespoons chocolate spread, and 1 teaspoon orange extract. Blend until smooth and pour into 3 tall glasses. Repeat to serve 6.

 2 Chocolate Orange Desserts

In a bowl, beat together 1 cup cream cheese or mascarpone cheese, 2 teaspoons finely grated orange rind, ½ cup Greek yogurt, and 3 tablespoons granulated sugar until smooth and thick. Stir in 3 oz finely chopped semisweet chocolate and spoon into 6 glass serving dishes. Chill for a minimum of 10 minutes. Meanwhile, mix 1½ cups crushed chocolate-coated graham crackers or cookies with 4 tablespoons melted butter. Spoon the cookie crumbs on top of the chocolate orange desserts to serve.

White Chocolate and Apricot Waffles

Serves 4

1¼ cups light cream
8 oz white chocolate
8 store-bought waffles
1 (15 oz) can apricot halves in juice
   or syrup, drained and sliced
pistachio nuts, crushed (optional)

- Pour the cream into a small saucepan and heat until hot, but not boiling. Meanwhile, finely chop or coarsely grate the white chocolate and place it in a heatproof bowl. Pour the hot cream over the chocolate and stir until the chocolate has melted and the mixture is smooth.

- Toast the waffles according to the package directions and arrange on serving dishes. Drizzle with a little cream and top with slices of apricot. Sprinkle with a few crushed pistachio nuts to decorate, if using, and serve with extra chocolate sauce.

 Poached Apricots Cut 8 apricots in half and remove their pits. Place in a saucepan with 1 cup water, 1 cup apple juice, 1 teaspoon vanilla extract (optional), and 2 tablespoons honey. Bring to a boil, then reduce the heat and simmer gently for 8–10 minutes, until tender. Pour into a large, shallow bowl and set aside to cool slightly. Meanwhile, make up the white chocolate sauce as above. Serve the poached apricots in attractive glass serving dishes, drizzled with the white chocolate sauce, if desired.

 White Chocolate and Apricot Muffins Place ½ cup granulated sugar in a large bowl with 1¾ cups all-purpose flour, 2 teaspoons baking powder, 3 oz white chocolate chunks, and ⅓ cup chopped dried apricots. In a separate bowl, beat 2 eggs with 4 tablespoons melted butter and ½ cup buttermilk or plain yogurt. Pour the liquid mixture into the dry ingredients and mix until barely combined. Divide the muffin mixture among the cups of a greased or paper cup-lined, 12-cup muffin pan and bake in a preheated oven, at 350°F, for 18–22 minutes, until risen and firm to the touch. Transfer to wire racks to cool and serve warm.

1 Berry-Full Baskets

Serves 6

1 cup (8 oz) mascarpone cheese

⅔ cup heavy cream

2 tablespoons granulated sugar

1 teaspoon vanilla extract
  (optional)

6 brandy snap baskets

4 cups mixed berries (such as
  hulled strawberries, raspberries,
  and blueberries)

- Beat together the mascarpone cheese, cream, granulated sugar, and vanilla, if using, until smooth and thick.

- Spoon into the brandy baskets and top with the mixed berries so that they are tumbling out. Serve immediately.

---

2 Very Berry Tarts

Unroll a sheet of store-bought rolled dough pie crust and use a 3½ inch plain or fluted pastry cutter to cut out 18 circles. Push into 18 cups in 2 tartlet pans and fill each one with 1 teaspoon mixed berry preserves. Bake in preheated oven, at 400°F, for about 12 minutes or until crisp and golden. Cool on a wire rack.

3 Berry Good Crisp

Mix 1 (1 lb) package frozen berries with 2 tablespoons packed light brown sugar and transfer to a buttered ovenproof dish. In a bowl, mix together ⅔ cup all-purpose flour and 6 tablespoons softened butter, rubbing with your fingertips until the mixture resembles bread crumbs. Stir in ¾ cup rolled oats and a small handful of slivered almonds (optional). Pour the topping mixture over the fruit and bake in a preheated oven, at 350°F, for about 20 minutes or until the topping is pale golden. Serve with cream or ice cream, if desired.

Chocolate Bar Brownie Cupcakes

Serves 4–6

8 oz semisweet chocolate

1 stick butter

2 extra-large eggs

½ cup firmly packed light
  brown sugar

⅔ cup all-purpose flour

½ cup baking powder

3 oz chocolate candy bar,
  cut into 12 slices

- Melt the semisweet chocolate with the butter in a small saucepan set over low heat until just melted.

- Meanwhile, whisk the eggs in a bowl with the sugar, then stir in the flour and baking powder. Pour in the melted chocolate mixture and stir to combine. Divide the batter among the cups of a greased or paper cup-lined, 12-cup cupcake pan. Push a slice of chocolate candy bar into each cupcake and bake in a preheated oven, at 350°F, for about 18 minutes or until almost firm to the touch. Cool in the pan until firm enough to handle. Serve warm or cold.

Chocolate Bar Fondue

Put 1 cup heavy cream and 4 oz each of chopped chocolate candy bar and semisweet chocolate in a bowl set over a saucepan of simmering water, stirring occasionally, until the chocolate has just melted. Pour into a small fondue pot set over a lit base following manufacturer's directions, then serve with a selection of sweet dippers, such as strawberries, chunks of banana, and marshmallows. (Or place the pan of water with the melted fondue bowl sitting on top directly onto a heatproof mat in the middle of the table.)

Milk Chocolate Chip Cookies

Beat 1 stick softened butter with ⅓ cup granulated sugar until pale and creamy. Beat in 1 egg yolk, then stir in 1 cup all-purpose flour, 1 tablespoon unsweetened cocoa powder, ½ teaspoon baking powder, and ½ cup milk chocolate chips until combined. Use your hands or 2 spoons to place slightly 16–20 flattened balls of the mixture on 2 baking sheets lined with parchment paper and bake in a preheated oven, at 350°F, for about 12 minutes, until slightly darker around the edges. Cool on wire racks.

Chewy Oat and Raisin Bars

Serves 6–8

1¾ sticks butter
⅓ cup light corn syrup or honey
½ cup sweetened condensed milk
⅔ cup granulated sugar
3½ cups rolled oats
½ cup raisins
⅔ cup all-purpose flour
½ cup baking powder

- Melt the butter with the corn syrup, condensed milk, and sugar in a large saucepan set over medium-low heat, then remove from the heat and stir in the oats, raisins, flour, and baking powder. Stir well.

- Scrape the batter into a 1½ inch deep, 10 inch square cake pan that has been greased and the bottom lined with parchment paper. Bake in a preheated oven, at 350°F, for 15–18 minutes, until pale golden.

- Remove from the oven and cool in the pan for 2–3 minutes before marking out and cutting about 16 squares or bars. Let cool for about 5 minutes or until cool and firm enough to handle, then transfer to a wire rack.

 Crunchy Strawberry, Oat, and Raisin Whip

Drop 1 tablespoon strawberry preserves into the bottom of each of 6 glass serving dishes or ramekins. Mix 1¼ cups strawberry yogurt with 1¼ cups crème fraîche or Greek yogurt and spoon it over the jam. Sprinkle a handful of crunchy oat and raisin granola cereal over the top and serve immediately.

 Coconut and Raisin Oat Cookies

In a bowl, beat together ½ cup granulated sugar and 1 stick butter until creamy, then add 2 tablespoons corn syrup, 1 small egg, ¾ cup all-purpose flour, ½ teaspoon baking powder, ¾ cup rolled oats, ½ cup raisins, and ¾ cup flaked dried coconut and mix until combined. Use 2 spoons to arrange about 20 slightly flattened spoonfuls

of the dough on 2 baking sheets lined with parchment paper. Cook in a preheated oven, at 350°F, for about 12 minutes, until golden. Remove from the oven and transfer to wire racks to cool.

Stewed Rhubarb with Custard

Serves 4–6

1½ lb rhubarb, cut into 1½ inch
   lengths (about 5½ cups)

3 tablespoons orange juice
   or water

½ teaspoon ground ginger
   (optional)

¼–½ cup granulated sugar

2 tablespoons custard powder
   or vanilla pudding mix

2½ cups milk

- Place the rhubarb in a large saucepan with the orange juice or water and ground ginger, if using. Reserve 1 tablespoon of the sugar and add as much of the remaining sugar as you like, depending on sweetness desired, to the rhubarb. Heat the pan until the sugar has dissolved, then simmer gently, stirring occasionally, for 6–8 minutes, until the rhubarb is tender. Remove from the heat and set aside to cool slightly.

- Meanwhile, place the custard powder in a bowl with the reserved sugar, then add 2 tablespoons of the milk and stir until it forms a paste. Heat the remaining milk in a saucepan until almost boiling, then pour into the paste in a steady stream, stirring constantly to prevent lumps from forming. Return to the pan and bring to boiling point, stirring constantly, until thickened. (Alternatively, heat 2½ cups store-bought vanilla pudding according to the package directions.)

- Spoon the rhubarb into bowls and serve with the custard.

 Rhubarb and Custard Sponge

Tart Beat 1¼ cups thick chilled custard or vanilla pudding into ½ cup mascarpone cheese and 1 teaspoon vanilla extract (optional) and spread thickly over a store-bought large yellow cake. Arrange 2 cups rhubarb pie filling over the cake. Cut into slices to serve.

 Roasted Rhubarb Crunch

Chop 1 lb rhubarb into 1½ inch lengths and mix in a large bowl with ¼ cup firmly packed light brown sugar, the finely grated rind and juice of 1 small orange, and ½ teaspoon ground ginger Transfer into a buttered, large ovenproof dish and cook in a preheated oven, at 375°F, for 15–20 minutes, until softened. Remove from the oven and set aside to cool slightly. Meanwhile, beat ½ cup mascarpone cheese into 1¼ cups chilled custard or vanilla pudding and 1 teaspoon vanilla extract (optional). Put 8 gingersnap cookies in a small freezer bag and tap with a rolling pin to break into coarse crumbs. Spoon the roasted rhubarb into dishes, top with a dollop of the mascarpone custard, and sprinkle with the crunchy cookie crumbs to serve.

STU-SWEE-FOK

30 Frozen Fruit Pie

Serves 4–6

1 (1 lb) package mixed frozen fruit

¾ cup granulated sugar

1 stick butter or margarine, softened

2 eggs

1 cup all-purpose flour

vanilla ice cream, to serve (optional)

- Transfer the frozen fruit into a buttered 8 x 10 inch shallow ovenproof dish with ¼ cup of the sugar.

- Put the remaining sugar, butter or margarine, eggs, and flour into a bowl and beat together until smooth. Spoon the mixture over the frozen fruits and smooth down evenly. Bake in a preheated oven, at 400°F, for 20–25 minutes, until risen and golden, then serve in bowls with vanilla ice cream, if desired.

---

1 **Frozen Fruit Cake Slices** Put 1 (1 lb) package frozen fruit into a saucepan with ¼ cup granulated sugar and warm over medium-low heat for 5–7 minutes, stirring occasionally, until the sugar has dissolved and the warm fruit begins to collapse. Meanwhile, cut a plain yellow cake into 4–6 slices and arrange on serving plates. Spoon the warmed fruit over the cake slices and serve immediately with a dollop of lightly whipped cream.

2 **Frozen Fruit Cupcakes** In a bowl, beat together ½ cup margarine and ⅔ cup granulated sugar, 1¼ cups all-purpose flour, 1 teaspoon baking powder, and 2 eggs until smooth. Gently fold 1 cup frozen fruit into the batter, then spoon into the cups of a greased or paper cup-lined, 12-cup cupcake pan. Bake in a preheated oven, at 400°F, for 12–14 minutes, until risen and pale golden. Serve warm with whipped cream or ice cream.

Chocolate Buttermilk Pancakes

Serves 4–6

1⅓ cups all-purpose flour, sifted
1 teaspoon baking powder
2 tablespoons granulated sugar
1 egg, lightly beaten
1 cup buttermilk
⅓ cup chocolate chips
butter, for cooking

To serve

whipped cream or ice cream
warm chocolate sauce (optional)

- Combine the flour in a bowl with the baking powder and sugar. Mix the egg into the buttermilk and pour the mixture into the dry ingredients. Beat together until you have a smooth, thick batter, then stir in the chocolate chips.

- Melt a small pat of butter in a large nonstick skillet and pour large tablespoonfuls of the batter into the skillet. Cook gently for 1–2 minutes, until bubbles begin to appear on the surface of the pancake, then carefully turn over and cook for about 1 more minute, until golden.

- Repeat with remaining batter, adding a little extra butter, if necessary.

- Serve with whipped cream or scoops of ice cream, drizzled with warmed chocolate sauce, if desired.

Hot Chocolate Custard Brownies

Pour 2 cups prepared custard or store-bought vanilla pudding into a small saucepan and warm gently until hot, but not boiling. Remove from the heat and stir in 3 oz chopped semisweet chocolate or ½ cup chocolate chips until melted. Meanwhile, arrange 4 chocolate brownies on serving dishes. Pour the hot custard over them to serve.

Saucy Chocolate Pudding

In a large bowl, beat 1 stick softened butter with ½ cup granulated sugar, 1¼ cups all-purpose flour, 1 teaspoon baking powder, 3 tablespoons cocoa powder, ½ cup milk, and 2 eggs until well combined. Scrape into a buttered ovenproof dish. Mix together ¼ cup granulated sugar, 1 tablespoon unsweetened cocoa powder, and ½ cup boiling water, then pour this mixture slowly over the batter in the dish. Bake in a preheated oven, at 350°F, for 18–20 minutes, until just firm to the touch. Serve with ice cream, if desired.

20 Apricot and Almond Tartlets

Serves 6

1 egg

¼ cup granulated sugar

4 tablespoons butter, softened

½ cup ground almonds
(almond meal)

6 (3¼ inch) baked individual
tart shells

6 apricot halves in juice, drained
and sliced

2 tablespoons slivered almonds

ice cream or whipped cream,
to serve (optional)

- In a bowl, beat the egg with the sugar, butter, and ground almonds until smooth and creamy. Divide the mixture between the pastry shells and top with the apricot slices.

- Sprinkle with the slivered almonds and bake in a preheated oven, at 350°F, for 12–15 minutes, until golden. Serve warm with a scoop of ice cream or a dollop of softly whipped cream, if desired.

Apricot and Amaretti Crisps

Drain 2 (15 oz) cans apricot halves in juice and mash with a fork until smooth. Spoon the mixture into 6 glasses. Whip 1 cup heavy whipping cream to soft peaks with 1 teaspoon vanilla extract (optional) and 2 tablespoons sifted confectioners' sugar. Spoon over the apricot puree, then crumble 3–4 amaretti cookies over each one and serve immediately.

Staples Apricot and Almond Crisp

Drain 2 (15 oz) cans apricot halves in juice, reserving the juice. coarsely slice the apricots and transfer to an ovenproof dish with 2 tablespoons of the reserved juice. Mix ½ cup chopped almonds into 1 cup all-purpose flour, 1 cup firmly packed brown sugar, and 4 tablespoons softened butter. Sprinkle the topping over the apricots and bake in a preheated oven, at 350°F, for 20–25 minutes, until golden.

10 Ice Cream with Rum and Raisin Syrup

Serves 2

2 tablespoons butter
¼ cup packed light brown sugar
2 tablespoons heavy cream
1 tablespoon dark rum
small handful of raisins
4 scoops of vanilla or rum and
    raisin ice cream, to serve

- Melt the butter in a small saucepan with the sugar and cream, stirring until dissolved. Add the rum and raisins, bring to a boil, then remove from the heat and set aside for the raisins to plump up and the sauce to cool slightly.

- Meanwhile, place 2 scoops of ice cream into bowls. Drizzle with the warm rum and raisin sauce to serve.

2 Rum, Raisin, and Pear Trifle

Heat 2 tablespoons coconut-flavored rum (such as Malibu) in a small saucepan with a small handful of raisins. Simmer gently for 1 minute, then remove from the heat and set aside until the are raisins plump. Meanwhile, divide 6 ladyfingers between 2 glass serving bowls. Drain 1 (15 oz) can pear halves in syrup or juice, reserving 2 tablespoons of the juice. Stir 2 tablespoons rum into the reserved juice and drizzle the mixture over the ladyfingers. Thickly slice the pear halves and layer over the sponge. Beat ⅔ cup Greek honey yogurt into ½ cup mascarpone cheese until smooth and thick, then spoon the mixture over the sliced pears. Sprinkle with the soaked raisins to serve.

3 Rum and Raisin Crepes with

Ice Cream Sift ⅔ cup all-purpose flour into a bowl with 1 tablespoon granulated sugar, creating a well or dip in the middle. Whisk 1 egg into 1 cup milk, then pour into the well and whisk to incorporate the flour from the edges until the batter is smooth. Set aside to rest for 10–15 minutes. Meanwhile, warm 3 tablespoons dark rum with 2 tablespoons granulated sugar, a small handful of raisins, 2 tablespoons butter, and 2 tablespoons water in a small saucepan set over medium-low heat. Stir to dissolve the sugar, then simmer gently for 2–3 minutes, until syrupy. Remove from the heat and set aside to cool slightly. Melt a small pat of butter in a skillet and pour enough of the batter into the skillet to thinly cover the bottom, swirling to coat the surface evenly. Cook for 1–2 minutes before carefully flipping over and cooking for another minute, or until golden and crispy. Remove and keep warm while you repeat the process, adding more butter when necessary, until all the batter has been used. Fold the crepes and arrange on warmed plates, topped with a scoop of ice cream, and drizzled with the rum and raisin syrup.

3️⃣ Warm Cranberry-Poached Pears

Serves 4–6

5 cups cranberry or cranberry
and apple juice

2 tablespoons honey

1 teaspoon vanilla extract
or seeds from 1 vanilla bean
(optional)

2 teaspoons lime or lemon juice

6 large Bosc pears

- Pour the cranberry juice into a large saucepan with the honey, vanilla extract or seeds, if using, and the lime or lemon juice and heat gently until it almost reaches boiling point.

- Meanwhile, peel and core the pears and cut them into quarters. Add to the pan and simmer gently for about 15 minutes, keeping the pears submerged in the poaching liquid, until tender. Remove from the heat and set aside to cool for about 10 minutes.

- Gently spoon the pears into serving bowls and ladle over some of the poaching liquid to serve.

 Crunchy Pear and Cranberry Desserts

Place ¾ cup rolled oats in a bowl with ½ cup chopped nuts, ¼ cup granulated sugar, and 4 tablespoons melted butter. Stir well to coat, then transfer to a large skillet and toast for 5–6 minutes, stirring frequently to prevent the mix from burning, until golden and crispy. Put into a shallow bowl to cool slightly, then stir in ½ cup dried cranberries. Arrange 2 drained pear halves in juice in each of 4–6 attractive serving dishes and sprinkle with the crunchy topping to serve.

 Quick Pear and Cranberry Crisp

Place ¾ cup rolled oats in a bowl with ½ cup chopped nuts, ¼ cup granulated sugar, and 4 tablespoons melted butter. Stir well to coat, then set aside. Drain 2 (15 oz) cans pear halves in juice, reserving 2 tablespoons of the juice. Dice the pears and put into a shallow ovenproof dish with ½ cup dried cranberries, the reserved juice, 1 tablespoon honey, and 1 teaspoon vanilla extract (optional). Sprinkle with the oat topping and bake in a preheated oven, at 350°F, for 12–15 minutes, until golden. Serve with ice cream, if desired.

30 Lemon Popping Candy Cupcakes

Serves 6

1 stick butter, softened

⅔ cup granulated sugar

1 cup all-purpose flour

1 teaspoon baking powder

2 eggs

1 tablespoon milk

2 teaspoons finely grated
  lemon rind

1¼ cups confectioners' sugar,
  sifted

2 teaspoons lemon juice

popping candy, to sprinkle

- In a large bowl, beat together the butter, sugar, flour, baking powder, eggs, milk, and 1 teaspoon of the lemon rind until pale and creamy.

- Divide the batter among the cups of a greased or paper cup-lined, 12-cup cupcake pan and bake in a preheated oven, at 375°F, for 12–15 minutes, until golden and risen. Cool on a wire rack.

- Meanwhile, mix the confectioners' sugar with the remaining lemon rind and just enough lemon juice to create a thick, smooth icing. Spread over the cold cupcakes and sprinkle with popping candy to serve.

 **Lemon Cupcake Surprise** Whip ⅔ cup heavy whipping cream to soft peaks with 1 teaspoon lemon rind and 1 tablespoon confectioners' sugar, sifted. Slice the tops off 12 store-bought lemon or vanilla cupcakes and dollop a scant teaspoon lemon curd onto each one. Top the curd with a spoonful of the whipped cream and sprinkle with a little popping candy, if desired. Replace the lids to serve.

Lemon Sorbet Cakes

Slice the tops off 6 store-bought lemon muffins and carefully remove a little of the innards from the bottom halves so that you can sit a scoop of lemon sorbet inside each one. Replace the tops and return to the freezer for 10 minutes. Meanwhile, gently heat ¼ cup granulated sugar in a small saucepan with 2 tablespoons water until dissolved, then increase the heat and simmer gently for 2–3 minutes, until syrupy. Remove from the heat and stir in 1 tablespoon lemon juice. Remove the muffins from the freezer, then drizzle the warm syrup over them and serve sprinkled with popping candy, if desired.

Mandarin and Meringue

Serves 6

2 cups heavy cream

1 teaspoon finely grated orange rind (optional)

3 oz store-bought meringues, broken into pieces

2 (11 oz) cans mandarin segments in juice, drained

- Whip the cream with the orange rind, if using, in a large bowl until soft peaks form.

- Fold in the meringues and mandarin segments, reserving a little of each to sprinkle over the tops. Spoon the mixture into bowls or sundae-style glasses and serve sprinkled with reserved meringue and mandarin.

White Chocolate Mandarin Nests

Melt 5 oz white chocolate in a bowl set over a saucepan of barely simmering water, making sure the bowl does not touch the surface of the water. Once the chocolate has melted, stir until smooth and set aside to cool slightly. Meanwhile, whip ⅔ cup heavy cream with 1 teaspoon finely grated lemon rind and divide among 6 meringue nests. Arrange the segments from 1 (11 oz) can mandarins, drained, over the filled meringue nests, then use a teaspoon to drizzle the melted chocolate over the top. Chill in the refrigerator for 4–5 minutes, until the chocolate has hardened, then serve immediately.

Upside-Down Mandarin Muffins

Divide half of 1 (11 oz) can mandarin segments, drained, among the cups of a greased or paper-cup lined, 12-cup muffin pan. In a large bowl, mix 2 cups all-purpose flour with 2 teaspoons baking powder, 1 teaspoon baking soda, ½ cup granulated sugar, and 1 teaspoon finely grated orange rind. In a small bowl, beat 1 egg with ⅓ cup vegetable oil and ⅔ cup buttermilk, then pour into the large bowl and mix gently with the dry ingredients until barely combined. Spoon the muffin batter into the prepared cups and bake in a preheated oven, at 350°F, for 18–22 minutes or until risen and firm to the touch.

Turn out of the muffins and serve upside down with light cream and the remaining mandarin segments.

Vanilla and Banana Yogurt

Serves 4

4 large ripe bananas

1 tablespoon honey

seeds from 1 vanilla bean or
1 teaspoon vanilla extract

2 cups vanilla yogurt, plus extra
to serve (optional)

fresh blueberries, to serve

- Peel and coarsely chop the bananas and place them in a bowl with the honey and vanilla seeds or vanilla extract.

- Mash the bananas until pulpy, then stir in the yogurt.

- Spoon the mixture into cups and serve sprinkled with fresh blueberries and extra yogurt, if desired.

Baked Bananas with Vanilla Cream

Cut a long slit along the length of 4 large, unpeeled bananas and drizzle 1 teaspoon honey into each one. Dot with 2 tablespoons diced butter, then wrap each banana individually in aluminum foil and bake in a preheated oven, at 400°F, for about 15 minutes, until the flesh is tender and the skin is blackened. Meanwhile, whip ⅔ cup heavy cream with the seeds from 1 vanilla bean or 1 teaspoon vanilla extract. Arrange the baked bananas on dishes and serve with the vanilla cream.

Vanilla and Banana Cakes

Beat 1 egg with 1 stick softened butter, ⅓ cup firmly packed light brown sugar, the seeds from 1 vanilla bean or 1 teaspoon vanilla extract, and 1 mashed, ripe banana. Fold in ¾ cup all-purpose flour and 1 teaspoon baking powder. Spoon into 8 cups of a greased or paper cup-lined, cupcake pan and bake in a preheated oven, at 350°F, for 18–20 minutes, until risen and golden. Remove from the oven, turn out onto serving dishes, and serve warm with cream.

10 Fresh Fruit Salad

Serves 6

1 small, ripe pineapple
1 small, ripe melon
2 cups strawberries
1 cup seedless grapes
2 tablespoons apple juice
  (optional)

- Cut the skin away from the pineapple, then slice into quarters and remove the hard core. Cut into bite-size chunks and place in a bowl, reserving any juices.

- Slice the melon in half and use a spoon to remove the seeds. Cut in half again and remove the skin from the flesh. Cut into bite-size pieces and add to the pineapple, again reserving any juices.

- Hull the strawberries, cutting them in half if necessary, and add to the prepared fruit along with the grapes.

- Mix the reserved juices with the apple juice, if using, and drizzle the liquid over the fruit. Toss gently to combine, then serve immediately.

2 Fruit Salad Tartlets

Brush 4 tablespoons melted butter over 6 sheets of phyllo pastry, then fold each sheet in half then in half again and push 1 into each of 6 cups of a muffin pan, folding down the edges to form 6 tartlets. Sprinkle with 2 tablespoons raw sugar. Bake in a preheated oven, at 375°F, for 8–10 minutes, until crisp and golden. Remove and cool on a wire rack. Once cold, spoon 2 tablespoons of store-bought vanilla pudding into each tartlet shell and divide 3 cups prepared mixed fruit chunks (such as strawberries, melon, grapes, and pineapple) among the tartlets to serve.

3 Fruit Salad Frozen Yogurt

Put 1 (1 lb) package of frozen fruit salad into a food processor with 2 cups fruit-flavored yogurt or plain yogurt and 2–3 tablespoons honey. Blend until just smooth and thick, then scrape into a shallow container and freeze for 25 minutes or until required.

Jelly Roll Cherry Bites

Serves 6

3 tablespoons granulated sugar
1 sheet ready-to-bake
   puff pastry
¼–⅓ cup cherry preserves or
   your favorite jam or preserves

- Sprinkle a clean work surface evenly with the granulated sugar and lay the pastry sheet over the sugar, pressing down to coat. Spread the preserves in a thin, even layer over the unsugared side of the pastry, then, starting with a long edge, roll up the pastry.

- Cut the pastry into 24 slices, each about ½ inch thick, and arrange on 2 baking sheets lined with parchment paper. Bake in a preheated oven, at 400°F, for 12–15 minutes or until crisp and golden. Carefully transfer to wire racks to cool slightly before serving.

Chocolate Cherry Jelly Roll Trifle

Arrange 1 small sliced chocolate jelly roll in a glass dish and pour 1 (15 oz) can cherry pie filling over the cake, then top with 1 cup prepared chocolate pudding. Softly whip ⅔ cup heavy whipping cream and spoon it over the pudding. Decorate with grated chocolate or chocolate curls, to serve.

Cherry Jelly Roll

Line and lightly grease a 13 x 9 inch jelly roll pan. Whisk 3 eggs in a bowl with ½ cup granulated sugar until pale and thick. Gently fold in ¾ cup all-purpose flour sifted with ¾ teaspoon baking powder and pour the batter into the prepared pan. Bake in a preheated oven, at 400°F, for 10–12 minutes, until golden and slightly springy to the touch. Meanwhile, lay a large piece of parchment paper on a clean dish towel and sprinkle the surface with about 2 tablespoons granulated sugar. Turn out the cake onto the sugared paper, then peel away the lining paper and roll up the cake tightly, using the dish towel to help. Let cool for 5 minutes, then gently unroll it and cool for another 2–3 minutes. Spread an even layer of black cherry preserves over the cake, then reroll and cut into slices to serve.

10 Apple and Ginger Crunch Cream

Serves 4

¾ cup mixed chopped nuts
1 teaspoon ground ginger
3 tablespoons granulated sugar
½ cup dry bread crumbs
4 tablespoons butter, melted
2 (15 oz) cans sliced apples, drained
1 cup crème fraîche or whipped cream

- Put the chopped nuts, ginger, sugar, and bread crumbs into a large skillet with the melted butter and cook over medium-low heat for 6–7 minutes, stirring constantly, until crisp and golden. Transfer to a large plate to cool.

- Meanwhile, divide the apple slices among 6 glass dishes and top each one with a dollop of crème fraîche. Spoon the crunchy topping over the top to serve.

 2 Apple and Ginger Baked Meringues

Drain 2 (15 oz) cans sliced apples and mix gently with 2 tablespoons packed brown sugar and 1 teaspoon ground ginger. Divide among 4 individual ovenproof dishes or ramekins. Whisk 1 extra-large egg white in a clean bowl until it stands in stiff peaks. Add ¼ cup granulated sugar, a spoonful at a time, whisking constantly. Spoon this mixture over the gingery apples and bake in a preheated oven, at 350°F, for 8–10 minutes, until pale golden. Serve immediately.

 3 Classic Ginger Cookies with Stewed Apple

Melt 1 stick butter with ½ cup light corn syrup over low heat, then set aside. Meanwhile, sift 2⅔ cups all-purpose flour, 2 teaspoons baking powder, 1 teaspoon baking soda, and 2 teaspoons ground ginger into a large bowl and stir in ¾ cup raw sugar. Pour the melted butter mixture into the bowl and mix well to combine, then use your hands to roll the mixture into about 20 balls. Arrange on 2 baking sheets lined with parchment paper, then flatten slightly and bake in a preheated oven, at 350°F, for 15–18 minutes, until golden and the surface is slightly cracked. Meanwhile, place 2 large peeled and sliced Granny Smith apples in a saucepan with 3 tablespoons packed brown sugar and a small splash of water. Cover and cook gently for about 10 minutes, stirring occasionally, until softened. Transfer the cookies to a wire rack to cool, then serve with bowls of the stewed apple and a dollop of crème fraîche or whipped cream, if desired. Store any leftover cookies in an airtight container.

Peachy Cinnamon Cheesecake

Serves 6

2 cups crushed graham crackers
  or cookies
1 teaspoon ground cinnamon
1 stick butter, melted
1⅔ cups cream cheese
½ cup peach-flavored yogurt
¾ cup confectioners' sugar, sifted
1 (15 oz) can peach halves in light
  syrup, drained and sliced

- In a large bowl, mix the cookie crumbs with half of the cinnamon and butter until well coated, then press the mixture into a 9 inch tart or cake pan. Chill in the refrigerator until required.

- Meanwhile, place the cream cheese and yogurt in a bowl and beat in the confectioners' sugar and remaining cinnamon until smooth and thick. Spoon the mixture over the cookie crust and smooth down evenly. Return to the refrigerator and chill for at least 20 minutes.

- Cut into wedges and serve with the sliced peaches.

 Peachy Cinnamon Smoothie

Put the contents of 1 (15 oz) can peaches in juice into a blender and add ½ teaspoon ground cinnamon, 1¼ cups chilled orange juice, and 2 peeled bananas. Blend until smooth, then pour into 3 glasses with ice cubes and repeat to serve 6.

 Cinnamon Pain Perdu with

Peaches In a large shallow bowl, whisk together 3 eggs plus 1 egg yolk, ⅔ cup granulated sugar, 1 teaspoon ground cinnamon, and 1¼ cups milk. Dip 3 thick slices of brioche or bread into the egg mixture, turning to coat. Melt 4 tablespoons butter in a large skillet and cook the brioche for about 2 minutes on each side until golden. Remove the pain perdu from the skillet and repeat the process with 3 more slices of brioche. Serve with freshly sliced peaches.

30 Raisin Sheet Cake

Serves 6

⅓ cup light corn syrup
1 stick butter, softened
1 cup all-purpose flour
1 teaspoon baking powder
⅔ cup granulated sugar
2 extra-large eggs
1 teaspoon vanilla extract
  (optional)
½ cup raisins
cream, whipped cream, or
  ice cream, to serve (optional)

- Pour the corn syrup into a greased 8 x 10 inch shallow ovenproof dish.

- Beat the remaining ingredients together until pale and creamy and spoon over the syrup coating. Bake in a preheated oven, at 400°F, for 20–25 minutes or until risen and golden.

- Serve with light cream, whipped cream, or ice cream, if desired.

1 Raisin Waffles

In a small saucepan, melt 2 tablespoons butter with ⅓ cup maple syrup or light corn syrup and ½ cup raisins until warm and melted. Meanwhile, toast 6 waffles until golden and arrange each one on a serving dish. Top with a scoop of vanilla ice cream and drizzle with the raisin syrup to serve.

2 Apple and Raisin Tart

Unroll a sheet of store-bought rolled dough pie crust and use it to line a 9 inch tart pan, trimming away excess dough around the edges. Prick the bottom with a fork, line with parchment paper, and cover the bottom with uncooked dried beans or rice. Bake in a preheated oven, at 350°F, for 12 minutes, then remove the paper and dried beans and return to the oven for another 5 minutes or until crisp and pale golden. (Alternatively, use a store-bought pie crust.) Meanwhile, peel, core, and slice 4 Pippin or Jonathan apples into thick wedges. Place in a large skillet with 4 tablespoons butter, ⅓ cup raisins, 2 tablespoons maple syrup or light corn syrup, ½ teaspoon ground cinnamon (optional), and 1 teaspoon lemon juice and cook gently for about 10 minutes, turning occasionally, until golden and tender. Scrape the apples into the pastry shell and serve with vanilla ice cream or cream.

1⏱ Easy Chocolate Sauce for Ice Cream

Serves 6–8

8 oz semisweet chocolate
3 tablespoons light corn syrup
2 tablespoons butter
½ cup heavy cream
vanilla ice cream with canned or
fresh fruit, to serve (optional)

- Place the chocolate, corn syrup, butter, and cream in a small saucepan set over low heat. (Alternatively, place in a bowl set over a saucepan of barely simmering water so that the bowl does not touch the surface of the water.) Melt the chocolate and butter gently, stirring until the mixture is smooth and glossy.

- Set aside to cool slightly, then drizzle it over vanilla ice cream and top with canned or fresh fruit, if desired.

2⏱ Easy Chocolate Cupcakes

In a large bowl, beat 2 eggs with 1 stick softened butter, ⅔ cup granulated sugar, ⅔ cup all-purpose flour, 1 teaspoon baking powder, and 1 heaping tablespoon unsweetened cocoa powder until pale and creamy. Fold in ½ cup chocolate chips, then divide the batter among the cups of a greased or paper cup-lined, 12-cup cupcake pan Bake in a preheated oven, at 375°F, for 12–14 minutes, until risen and golden. Transfer to wire racks to cool slightly before serving.

3⏱ Easy Chocolate Cake

In a large bowl, beat together 1½ sticks of softened butter, ¾ cup granulated sugar, 1⅓ cups all-purpose flour, 2 teaspoons baking powder, 2 tablespoons sifted unsweetened cocoa powder, and 3 extra-large eggs until pale and creamy. Divide between two 8 inch cake pans that have been greased and the bottoms lined with parchment paper. Bake in a preheated oven, at 375°F, for 20–22 minutes, until risen and firm to the touch. Remove from the oven, turn out onto cooling racks, and peel away the paper lining. Once cold, sandwich together with your choice of store-bought frosting and serve in wedges. Alternatively, serve the cake warm with ice cream and drizzled with the easy chocolate sauce.

Index

Acknowledgments

Recipes by: Jo McAuley
Executive Editor: Eleanor Maxfield
Senior Editor: Leanne Bryan
Copy Editor: Salima Hirani
Americanizer: Theresa Bebbington
Art Direction: Tracy Killick Art Direction and Design
Original Design Concept: www.gradedesign.com
Designer: Tracy Killick for Tracy Killick Art Direction and Design
Photographer: William Shaw
Home Economist: Joy Skipper
Prop Stylist: Liz Hippisley
Assistant Production Manager: Caroline Alberti